Chopin: his life and times

CHOPIN

his life and times

Ateş Orga

MIDAS BOOKS

B
C5490
c.1

By the same author
The Proms
Records and Recording Classical Guide 77 (editor)

To my wife Josephine, a token of things shared

In the same illustrated documentary series

General Editor: Ateş Orga

HAYDN	Neil Butterworth
MOZART	Peggy Woodford
VERDI	Peter Southwell-Sander
BEETHOVEN	Ateş Orga (in preparation)
MENDELSSOHN	Mozelle Moshansky (in preparation)
RACHMANINOV	Robert Walker (in preparation)
WAGNER	Derek Elley (in preparation)
TCHAIKOVSKY	Wilson Strutte (in preparation)
ELGAR	Eric Roseberry (in preparation)
SCHUBERT	Peggy Woodford (in preparation)
PUCCINI	Peter Southwell-Sander (in preparation)
ROSSINI	Peter Southwell-Sander (in preparation)
LISZT	Mozelle Moshansky (in preparation)
DVOŘÁK	Neil Butterworth (in preparation)

First published in 1976 by
MIDAS BOOKS,
12 Dene Way, Speldhurst,
Tunbridge Wells, Kent TN3 0NX

Revised 2nd Edition 1978
© Ateş D'Arcy-Orga 1976 and 1978
ISBN 0 85936 116 0 (U.K. Casebound Edition)
ISBN 0 8467 0416 1 COMA (U.S. Paperbound Edition)

All rights reserved. No part of this publication may be reproduced, stored in a retrieval system, or transmitted, in any form or by any means, electronic, mechanical, photocopying, recording or otherwise, without the prior permission of Midas Books

Printed in Great Britain by
Chapel River Press, Andover, Hants.

Contents

Acknowledgments

I would like to acknowledge here the help and encouragement of the late Arthur Hedley and Maurice J. E. Brown, who when they were alive brought a rare and exhilarating standard of scholarship to modern Chopin research. My thanks must also go to Adam Harasowski, Baron Sachlan Linden (for some pertinent suggestions), and my publishers, Kathleen and Ian Morley-Clarke, for their enthusiasm and support. And, of course, I have to thank my wife for her advice (and her infinite patience), as well as my late parents and especially my father who tolerated my efforts for so long and who was the first to help me with this book when it was first planned in the mid-sixties.

My thanks must also go to the following for kindly granting permission to quote extracts:

   Barrie Books Ltd (Alan Walker, *Chopin*)
   Free Press of Glencoe/Collier-Macmillan Ltd (Liszt, *Frédéric Chopin*, trans. Edward N. Waters)
   Victor Gollancz Ltd (Berlioz, *Memoirs,* trans. David Cairns)
   Adam Harasowski/Hansom Books Ltd ("Death and auction in Paris")
   Weidenfeld & Nicolson (Eleanor Perényi, *Liszt*)

Most of the illustrations have come from my own collection or from original prints and engravings. Grateful thanks, however, are due to the following for kindly granting reproduction rights:

   Beethoven-Haus, Bonn
   Bibliothèque du Conservatoire de Musique, Paris
   Bibliothèque Nationale, Paris
   British Museum, London
   Carnavalet Museum, Paris
   Chopin Institute, Warsaw
   Historisches Museum, Vienna
   Mickiewicz Museum, Warsaw

Original spellings have been retained for most names in this book, with the exception of the more familiar Gallic versions of Chopin's own name and those of his sisters.

Wadhurst, December 1976   *A.O.*

Bibliography

Abraham, Gerald, *Chopin's Musical Style* (Oxford 1939)

d'Agoult, Marie *Mémoires, 1833-54,* ed. Daniel Ollivier (Paris 1927)

Berlioz, Hector *Memoirs,* rev. Ernest Newman (New York 1932)
— *Memoirs,* trans. David Cairns (London 1969)

Bourniquel, Camille *Chopin* (New York, London 1960)

Branson, David *John Field and Chopin* (London 1972)

Brown, Maurice J. E. *Chopin: an Index of his works in chronological order* (London 1960, rev. ed.1972)

Chissell, Joan *Chopin* (London 1965)

Hallé, Charles *Autobiography,* ed. Michael Kennedy (London 1972)

Harasowski, Adam *The Skein of Legends around Chopin* (Glasgow 1967)
— "Death and auction in Paris", *Music & Musicians,* Vol. XVII/vi (February 1969)

Hedley, Arthur *Chopin* (London 1947)
— *Selected Correspondence of Fryderyk Chopin* (London 1962)

Iwaszkiewicz, Jaroslaw *Chopin* (Warsaw 1956)

Jonson, E. Ashton *A Handbook to Chopin's Works* (London 1905)

Kobylańska, Krystyna *Chopin in his own Land* (Cracow 1955; in English)
— *Chopin na obczyźnie* (Cracow 1965)

Liszt, Franz *Frédéric Chopin,* trans. Edward N. Waters (New York 1963)

Niecks, Frederick, *Frederick Chopin as Man and Musician* (London 1888)

Opieński, Henryk *Chopin's Letters* (London 1932)

Perényi, Eleanor *Liszt* (New York 1974; London 1975)

Schumann, Robert *Music and Musicians: Essays and Criticisms,* trans. Fanny Raymond Ritter (New York 1876)

Walker, Alan (ed.) *Chopin: Profiles of the Man and the Musician* (London 1966)

Wierzynski, Casimir *The Life and Death of Chopin* (London 1951)

Frontispiece (and cover). Chopin. From an oil painting by Eugène Delacroix, 1838 (Louvre, Paris)

Chapter 1

Childhood

'Less a musician than a susceptible soul' — *The Illustrated London News*
(after Balzac)

Legends are made, heroes are born. They seldom die. They are the
stuff of history, of imagination. They are man's inheritance, his
legacy. They are the inspiration of the future. Frédéric François
Chopin, albeit a musician, was such a legend, such a hero. One of
Poland's great sons he became synonymous with Poland itself. His
mazurkas and polonaises became the spirit incarnate of the Polish
people and the Polish steppe. Years after his death his music had
lost none of its alchemic genius or its magical influence. For
countless millions it even came to be a symbol of freedom and
liberation, and no more so perhaps than for those Poles during the
last World War who remembered that Chopin himself had penned
most of it as an exile in Paris while Russia's invading might held the
motherland. When Szymanowski's brother-in-law, Jaroslaw
Iwaszkiewicz, published his life of Chopin in Warsaw in 1956, he
probably summed-up better than most what Chopin has come to
mean today:

> His work has remained, to endure and increase in its scope and
> influence with the passage of time, entering ever more intimately
> into the lives of men, revealing new riches every day, and growing
> every day more and more indispensable. It expresses the struggles
> and the suffering of every one of us and forms a rainbow bridge
> between Poland and the rest of the world. It remains as the finest
> art Poland has ever produced.

Chopin was born in the village of Zelazowa Wola, to the west of
Warsaw, on 1 March 1810. His birthplace is still standing, today a
museum dedicated to his memory. Long and low, with flowers and
rambling plants surrounding the windows and porch, it reposes in
a large garden. A group of tall trees offers shade and relieves the
monotony of the plains that stretch to the horizon. A stream flows
nearby, in the heat of summer murmuring softly, a haven of cool
rest, in winter, frozen and silent. In Chopin's day the house
belonged to the Skarbek family and it was the Skarbeks who
employed Chopin's father, Nicholas, as a tutor to their children.

[handwritten margin note: date is not confirmed]

9

Nicholas was born in 1771 in the village of Marainville which nestled among the sunny vine-growing provinces of Lorraine in eastern France. The son of peasant stock, his father (a wheelwright by trade) and grandfather both owned extensive vineyards, and the family appears to have been long established in the area. When Nicholas was a boy, his village belonged to a Polish nobleman, Michel Pac, who may have come to the area when Stanislaus I, King of Poland, was made Duke of Lorraine in 1735. Nicholas was thus familiar with Poles from an early age, and was popular with several members of Pac's staff, including Adam Weydlicj, who was responsible for organising and running the count's estates.

Nicholas was markedly more intelligent than the rest of his family, whose intellectual poverty — the women could neither read nor write — must have stifled much of his enthusiasm for life, and his desire to broaden his experiences and become a man of the world. So when he was sixteen he took the opportunity to travel to Poland with Adam Weydlicj, whom he had begun to help in the administration of Michel Pac's affairs and business. Young as he was, he was highly regarded and trusted by his superiors. He became adept at dealing with financial problems, and his command of Polish and French, and later German, stood him in good stead, as well as being remarkable achievements for someone of his humble origins.

Nicholas liked the atmosphere he found in Warsaw and used his talent with figures to become an apprentice clerk in a tobacco factory. So long, too, as he remained in Poland, he avoided conscription into the French army, and this was crucial since at that time France was a nation seething with unrest and on the verge of the most epic revolution in modern history. In the only surviving letter which has come down to us (15 September 1790) Nicholas observed that 'being in a foreign country where I can pursue my own small career I should be sorry to leave it to become a soldier, even if it were for my country'. Ultimately though he was not to be spared the stresses and suffering of the French Revolution, for the symbol it represented — democratic freedom — became an example for the rest of Europe. Poland, a country divided since 1772 between Russia, Prussia and, later, Austria, needed little encouragement to follow suit — with the result that one day in the spring of 1794 Nicholas found his daily routine dramatically interrupted when the Polish National Guard staged an uprising to resist and overthrow the occupying armies of Catherine the Great of Russia. By now Nicholas was more and more committed to the Polish cause, and was rapidly losing interest in France. He joined the National Guard under their leader, Kościuszko, distinguished himself and rose to the rank of captain. But the revolt was crushed, and Warsaw was allocated to the Prussians. Nicholas was despondent. He had no money, the tobacco factory no longer existed, and he thought of returning to France. Illness, however, prevented him from doing so: 'Twice I

Chopin's birthplace
(Chopin Institute,
Warsaw)

have tried to leave', he said, 'and twice I have nearly died. I must bow before the will of providence and I will stay'. His decision was so final that he severed what tenuous links there were with his homeland and in later years kept all knowledge from his children of his French birthright and plebeian beginnings. He even declared France to be a 'foreign' country.

For the first few years Nicholas' fluent command of French and Polish proved useful and he became tutor to the children of various aristocratic families, finally accepting a post with the Skarbeks in 1802. Here he met his future wife, Justyna, a quiet, well-educated girl in her early twenties, a daughter of a farmer, and a poor relation of the wealthy Skarbeks. She was lady-in-waiting to the Countess, and was said to have played the piano well. She evidently enchanted Nicholas, who had an ear for good music and himself played the flute and violin. They were married in June 1806 and had four children: Louise, Frédéric, Isabella and Emilia. Isabella, always intensely proud of her brother's gift, lived the longest—she died in 1881—while Emilia was claimed by consumption at the age of fourteen. Louise, emotionally and temperamentally close to Frédéric, died some six years after him.

The young Chopin was a sensitive and poetic child, qualities he inherited from his mother, and he was brought up in

Above Right. Chopin's
parents – Justyna
(1782-1861) and Nicholas
(1771-1844).
Drawing by Ambrozy
Miroszewski, 1829
Above. Louise Chopin
(1807-55). Painting by
Miroszewski, 1829

Warsaw—then little more than a provincial town—where his
parents had moved shortly after his birth. His father held the post
of Professor of French at the Lyceum (High School) but later had
to take other posts as a French teacher in order to meet the cost of
living a life of pleasant material richness in the most fashionable
part of the city. During these early years Warsaw was still part of
the Grand Duchy of Warsaw formed by Napoleon in 1807. To the
young Chopin the Napoleonic example meant little, although it
coloured and shaped an era. Terror and tragedy smouldered on
distant horizons, Napoleon's armies marched bravely on doomed
campaigns, but Warsaw remained an isolated centre of peace and
solitude, a watershed of Europe. By 1814-15, when the Congress of
Vienna met to re-organise a broken Europe, Poland was divded yet
again between Austria, Russia and Prussia, and Warsaw became
the capital of the region controlled by the Russians who had
re-occupied the city in 1813.

His father's shrewd judgement and sense of logic were important
in moulding Chopin, whose upbringing and family environment
ensured, too, that he was well mannered, with all the social graces.
He was an aristocrat by nature, something which later never
ceased to surprise his contemporaries. In those days, it must be
remembered, musicians were regarded as little more than
servants, a legacy of earlier times when composers like J.S. Bach,
Domenico Scarlatti or Haydn were in the employment of rich
patrons or the church. They supplied music to demand, a
commodity for entertainment or special occasions. In the 19th
century, following the example of Beethoven, musicians were
freeing themselves from such bondage, but audiences, often
exclusively made up of royalty and the aristocracy, still viewed
them with some disdain. In their view a mere 'piano player'—who
exploited his art with the showmanship of a trapeze artist—was a

common entertainer, an occupation which no 'gentleman' of Chopin's distinction and manner would even consider.

Chopin's passionate love of music showed itself at an early age. There are stories, for instance, of how when his mother and Louise played dances on the grand piano (a luxury, for most families had only small or square instruments in those days) he would burst into tears for the sheer beauty and fragility of the sounds he heard. Soon he began to explore the keyboard for himself and delighted in experimenting. By the age of seven he had become sufficiently good for his parents to try and find him a teacher. Their choice fell on Adalbert Zywny, a Bohemian composer then aged sixty-one and now remembered solely as Chopin's first teacher.

He was a competent person, who for five years instilled into Chopin an everlasting admiration and reverence for the works of Bach and Mozart. He also encouraged him to explore the music of the great Viennese composers, as well as more fashionable pieces by lesser men, and gave him a solid grounding in the rudiments of music. Zywny's approach was ideally affectionate and understanding.

In spite of Zywny's teaching, however, Chopin had a will of his own: in practising the piano he amused himself more with improvisation and making up pieces, than in the playing of scale or finger exercises (though later, as a teacher himself, he put great belief in such systematic practice). His father once wrote that 'the

Above. Isabella Chopin (1811-81). Painting by Miroszewski, 1829

Below. Warsaw. Steel engraving by Adam Piliński

13

Adalbert Zywny
(1756-1842). Painting
by Mirozsewski

mechanism of playing took you little time, and your mind rather than your fingers were busy. If others spent whole days struggling with the keyboard you rarely spent a whole hour at it...'

Within a few months of beginning his studies with Zywny, Chopin began to play in public, and by the end of 1817 had already been described in the diary of one Alexandra Tańska as 'Mozart's successor'. As an infant prodigy of only seven he enjoyed wide popularity, but his extreme youth prevented him from becoming conceited or vain. After his first major concert, on 24 February 1818, when he played a Gyrowetz concerto in aid of charity, his only thoughts, it is said, were not for his talent but for his velvet jacket and collar and what the audience thought of them. He soon came to the attention of several distinguished Polish families, including the Radziwills and Potockis, and for one so young remained seemingly unspoilt in spite of all the excitement and praise. Meanwhile, his father ensured that his son's general education was not suffering and until the age of thirteen Chopin studied at home under his supervision. Always cautious, Nicholas had no wish to see the young Chopin follow the fate of so many other prodigies.

In the first few months of his lessons with Zywny, Chopin also began to compose, and in November 1817 a short Polonaise in G minor, was published. The same year saw the appearance of a Military March, which so impressed the Grand Duke Constantine that he ordered it to be scored for band and performed. Although it was published no copies seem to have survived, and the original manuscript — almost certainly written out by Zywny — is similarly lost. Several other pieces also appeared and they began to show that Chopin's real creative gifts lay in music rather than anything else. It is interesting to note, however, that even before he began composition he had already penned various formal verses as tokens of greeting for his parents' namedays. This one, written for his father on 6 December 1816, is, if nothing else, a worthy feat for a child of only six:

> When the world declares the festivity of your nameday,
> my papa, it brings joy to me also, with those wishes;
> that you may live happily, may not know grievous care,
> that God may always favour you with the fate you desire—
> these wishes I express for your sake.

Just two years later, however, Chopin was to write to his father that he could express his 'feelings more easily if they could be put into notes of music...' (6 December 1818).

Despite this total involvement with music, and his impressionable contact from an early age with the poets, writers and artists who used to meet in his father's house, Chopin was by no means pompous or dull in his outlook on life. He was, in fact, active and boisterous and hardly the 'frail and sickly' boy described by Liszt in his largely erroneous biography of Chopin, published many years later. He had, too, a sense of humour and devastating

Emilia Chopin
(1813-27). Miniature,
anonymous

mimicry, a witty philosophy, and a healthy interest in mixing with his companions, often the children of noblemen. As he grew older he skated (once cracking his head on the ice) and delighted in flirting with the girls, sometimes to the consternation of his father. When he was fourteen he wrote to his close school friend, Wilhelm Kolberg: 'You're not the only one that rides, for I can stick on, too. Don't ask how well, but I can—enough for the horse to go slowly wherever he prefers while I sit fearfully on his back like a monkey on a bear. Until now I haven't had any falls because the horse hasn't thrown me off: but, if ever he should want me to tumble off, I may do it some day' (19 August 1824). A year later he remarked to his parents that his 'health was as good as a faithful dog', and in these years Chopin was indeed the happiest and most keenly observant of children.

By this time he had left Zywny and become a pupil at the Warsaw Lyceum, beginning in the autumn of 1823. He had started his formal education. For the next three years music had to take second place. His Latin and Greek were good but, for all his efforts, his spelling refused to improve, and to the end of his life he continued to mis-spell foreign words. During the long hot summers of Central Europe, he would go for his holidays to the country estates of his friends. Here, away from Warsaw, he began to come under the influence of the Polish peasants and their music. This was first revealed in the columns of a 'newspaper' which he and his sister, Emilia, compiled during their summer holidays of 1824, called the *Szafrania Courier*. This was written in the long since ruined castle of the Dziewanowski family, whose son, Dominick, was at school with Chopin. In this 'newspaper' Chopin's awareness of nature, his outlook on life, and his interest in national music were all vividly communicated. Observing the dance step and rhythms of the mazurka and other regional music—which he learnt to dance with expert fluency—Chopin found time to experiment and sketched several pieces which he later developed into a body of memorable piano miniatures. In the salons and ballrooms of the Warsaw aristocracy he similarly came under the spell of the stately and festive polonaise with which he so readily identified himself, once remarking that he would make changes to the polonaise form until his death, a prophecy amply borne out.

1825 was a year crucial in determining Chopin's future. In May he was invited to demonstrate a novel kind of piano-organ, called the Aeolomelodikon, in the Great Hall of the Warsaw Conservatoire. He made a good impression with his improvisation and played a piano concerto by Moscheles, a fashionable composer who was one of the early influences on his music. A few days later, Alexander I, Tsar of Russia and brother of the Grand Duke Constantine, commanded Chopin to demonstrate the new Aeolomelodikon and presented him with a diamond ring in token of the occasion. (It may be noted in passing that this was not actually Chopin's first encounter with the illustrious: in the space

of only a few years he had been presented to the Tsar's mother, the Empress Maria Teoderowna when she visited Warsaw in September 1818, and a year later had played for the great Italian soprano, Angelica Catalani, who gave him an inscribed gold watch.)

On 2 June, a few days after he had played to the Tsar, the *Warsaw Courier* announced the publication of Chopin's first official work, the Rondo in C minor, Op. 1, which was dedicated to his headmaster's wife. The rondo helped consolidate the impression made before the Tsar, and the warm praise of the influential Prince Antoine Radziwill together with the appreciation of a leading German music magazine, the Leipzig *Allgemeine Musikalische Zeitung,* were enough to convince Chopin's parents that their son was intended for a musical career. Considering his previous work, the rondo was an astonishingly fluent achievement for a fifteen year old, although by now he had not only been studying textbooks on harmony and counterpoint but, since leaving Zwyny in 1822, had also been taking some private lessons with Josef Elsner, Director of the Warsaw Conservatoire, founded in 1821. Strangely, the elation Chopin must have felt at seeing such an important work in print is not preserved in any of the letters of the period that are still extant.

Chopin's last year at the Lyceum concentrated on general subjects: his father was anxious that he should acquit himself well in the classics and mathematics. During this academic year Chopin was made organist of the school ('The most important person in the whole Lyceum, after his reverence the priest!', he wrote in November), and although he never composed for the organ, it was an instrument that left its influence in some of his music, and of which he had a complete technical mastery. He frequently accompanied and extemporised at the Convent of the Visitation in Warsaw, often in a most daring fashion, and several of his contemporaries left glowing accounts of his organ playing. After leaving Poland, however, he seldom touched the instrument.

Christmas of that year was spent in the snow covered surrounds of Chopin's birthplace. Back in Warsaw in 1826 his last minute preparations for the summer examinations left little time for either correspondence or music. But in the late spring he remembered with some regret that 'my Botanical Gardens [belonging to the Kazimierzowski Palace where Chopin had spent many happy hours as a child]... have been beautifully done up by the Commission [as part of a general effort to modernise the city]. There are no more carrots that used to be so nice to eat beside the spring — nor sandwiches, nor arbours, nor salads, nor cabbages nor bad smells: only flower beds in the English style' (15 May).

Chopin had devoted so much time and energy to his general studies that when examination time arrived in the July he was quite exhausted and the strain of sitting the exams proved too much for him. For the first time he was ill, his finely sculptured face, with

Josef Elsner (1769-1854). Lithograph by Maximilian Fajans, Warsaw 1851

17

the beautiful eyes of his mother and the aquiline nose of his father, at times assuming that hollow, gaunt appearance which became so prominent and haunting in later years. At the end of the month, however, hearing that he had pased the examinations successfully, he was able to relax. On the evening of the presentation day, 27 July, he went to the Warsaw Opera with Wilhelm Kolberg to hear Rossini's *La Gazza Ladra,* and that same evening wrote a polonaise incorporating one of Kolberg's favourite melodies from the opera.

The following day he went for a well earned rest to Reinertz, a Silesian mineral spa in the west of Poland, accompanied by his mother and his sisters, Louise and Emilia. Emilia was already seriously unwell, and no amount of rest or remedies could cure her. She died the following spring.

The visit to Reinertz proved dull and uneventful: 'They say I am

Chopin's birthplace in winter. Photograph by Adam Kaczkowski

Chopin. Pencil
drawing by Eliza
Radziwill, 1826

looking a little better, but I am said to be getting fat and am as lazy
as ever,' he observed to Kolberg on 18 August. He had to endure
tedious timetables for his own cure, and the only real pleasure he
obtained was in taking long walks by himself in the hills
surrounding the spa: 'Often I am so delighted with the view of
these valleys that I hate to come down'.

Chapter 2

At the Warsaw Conservatoire

'Chopin's variations are constantly running through my head'—
Schumann (as Florestan)

Back in Warsaw in the September of 1826, Chopin was at least free
to follow the dictates of his heart, and was duly enrolled for three
years as a student of the Warsaw Conservatoire. He studied with
Elsner, whose methods he already knew. While Elsner, himself a
successful if 'academic' composer, was observant enough not to
impose his will on Chopin, he must have been often irritated
during the first two years by Chopin's weak attempts at musical
theory, counterpoint, harmony, orchestration and set composition. Chopin, however, found his best expression came in
individual and original pieces written solely for the piano. For him
the rigorous practice of writing fugues, masses or chamber music
was a drudgery; he was not interested in such formalised
composition, and his exercises were often outright failures. It was
difficult, too, to channel his thoughts into pre-determined,
stereotyped musical forms or procedures. He was more concerned
to get on with *his* kind of music. Any alternative produced inferior
results and there is a good illustration of this in the apprentice First
Piano Sonata, dedicated dutifully to Elsner. Yet even here there
are moments when he seeks to depart from the requirements laid
down by his teacher (not least in the 5/4 slow movement).
Ironically many of the 'rules' Chopin had to follow so reluctantly
were themselves, of course, the product of arbitrary decisions put
forward by the teachers of the day, and had no precedent in the
great classical works of Bach and Mozart which he had worshipped
since a boy. In a period when textbook formulae were considered
more important than the example of actual music, Chopin's
dilemma was pitiful.

If Chopin found life difficult under his teachers, he was in his
spare time able to experiment and write music as he pleased.
Nobody restricted his freedom and natural curiosity, or
questioned his techniques. Among his more interesting pieces was
a *Rondo à la Mazur*. This was notable for an early use of the
sharpened fourth degree characteristic of the Lydian mode (that is

John Field
(1782-1837). Steel
engraving attributed to
Carl Mayer

to say, the note F sharp — not F — in the scale of C major), which was related to the melodic inflexions of Polish folk music. In later years Chopin was to cleverly integrate such traits with his mature language.

From 1827 dates Chopin's first Nocturne (in E minor, Op. 72, No. 1), a form he made uniquely his own, adapting it from the examples of John Field. Field was an Irish composer, a pupil of Clementi, who had settled in St. Petersburg. His delicate, refined piano music and concertos influenced many 19th century composers, and Liszt, in his preface to an early edition of the nocturnes published in Paris in 1859, has left us a vivid account of his admiration:

> The charm which I have always found in these pieces, with their wealth of melody and refinement of harmony, goes back to the years of my earliest childhood. Long before I dreamed of ever meeting their creator, I had given myself up for hours at a time to the soothing influences of the visions flowing from the gentle intoxication of this music.

Later in this same essay on Field, Liszt summed up Chopin's

21

development of the genre in a language that is full of that exuberance and colour which was so typical of the age in which he lived:

> Even under the names of Nocturnes, we have seen the shy, serenely tender emotions which Field charged them to interpret, supplanted by strange and foreign effects. Only one genius possessed himself of this style, lending to it all the movement and ardour of which it was susceptible, yet preserving all its tenderness and the poising flight of its aspirations. Filling the entire scope of elegiac sentiment, and colouring his reveries with the profound sadness for which Youth found some chords of so dolorous vibration, Chopin, in his poetic Nocturnes, sang not only the harmonies which are the source of our most ineffable delights, but likewise the restless, agitating bewilderment to which they often give rise. His flight is loftier, though his wing be more wounded: and his very suaveness grows heart-rendering, so thinly does it veil his despairful anguish. We may never hope to surpass—which, in the arts, means to equal—that pre-eminence of inspiration and form with which he endowed all the pieces he published under this title. Their closer kinship to sorrow than those of Field renders them the more strongly marked; their poetry is more sombre and fascinating; they ravish us more, but are less reposeful, and thus permit us to return with pleasure to those pearly shells that open, far from the tempests and the immensities of the Ocean, beside some murmuring spring shaded by the palms of a happy oasis which makes us forget even the existence of the desert.

By far the most important of Chopin's early student works, however, was the set of Variations on *Là ci darem la mano* from Mozart's opera, *Don Giovanni,* for piano and orchestra, written during the summer holidays of 1827. The theme which Chopin used as the basis of his work was one which attracted many composers, who wrote several *brillante* fantasias on it, but Chopin's was a substantial musical achievement, seeking to combine careful thought with virtuoso display. This was such an important work—a considerable improvement on the Rondo, Op. 1—that after it was published, Clara Wieck (who later married Schumann) became the first pianist, other than the composer, to play it in public. The 21-year old Schumann was so impressed that he wrote in a now famous review, published in December 1831 in the Leipzig *Allgemeine Musikalische Zeitung,* 'Off with your hats, gentlemen—a genius... I bend before Chopin's spontaneous genius, his lofty aim, his mastership!' It was the first serious appreciation of Chopin as a composer.

The following year, 1828, saw Chopin widening his experiences. Musical life in Warsaw centred almost entirely around the Opera, and the staple fare was Rossini, whose music had swept Europe off its feet. Chopin was equally enthusiastic, using (as we have noted) Rossini's popular tunes in his own works, but such a diet inevitably became boring and when the composer, pianist and teacher, Hummel, visited Warsaw in the early part of 1828, Chopin seized the opportunity of hearing him perform. He was

Gioacchino Rossini
(1792-1868). Etching,
anonymous, 1820

soon inspired by Hummel's music and style of piano playing, which
combined a classical simplicity — he had been a pupil of Mozart,
Haydn and Clementi — with a romantic intensity and dexterity of
fingerwork, foreshadowing features in Chopin's own work.
Chopin, of course, did not hesitate to make Hummel's
acquaintance, and Hummel was probably the first widely
recognised composer of the period with whom he came into
contact.

Later that year, after his summer holidays, Chopin made his
first excursion away from Poland. A colleague of his father's had to
attend a zoological conference in Berlin and invited Chopin to
accompany him. Berlin, capital of Prussia under their king,
William Frederick III, was the centre of a flourishing musical life.
Ever since the end of the 17th century, during the time of the
Electors of Brandenburg, opera, in particular, was held in high
esteem. Berlin in the late 18th century saw performances of such
classic masterpieces as Mozart's *Seraglio, Le Nozze di Figaro* and
Don Giovanni, while in 1821, after a long and bitter struggle
against the predominance of imported Italian opera, the German

23

Johan Nepomuka
Hummel (1778-1837).
Lithograph by
Charles-Louis Constans

nationalist school triumphed with the first performance of
Weber's *Der Freischütz* at the State Opera. The king, however,
was a lover of spectacle, and fashionable Italian operas — which
had this quality — were still a main part of the musical life in the
city.

Chopin may have been out of his element in the company of
learned scientists — whom he frequently caricatured in his letters —
but eagerly immersed himself in the abundance of new 'celebrity'
music which he heard. On one occasion he encountered Handel's
Ode for St. Cecilia's Day for soloists, chorus and orchestra, and this
made a profound impression: he wrote to his family on 20
September that it 'is nearer to the ideal that I have formed of great
music'. Strange to ponder that with this early love of opera and
sacred music, Chopin himself cultivated a vastly different form of
musical expression.

While in Berlin, Chopin once found himself in the presence of
Mendelssohn, but 'I felt shy about introducing myself'. Although
Mendelssohn was only a year older he was much more a man of the
world, with the overture *A Midsummer Night's Dream,* and a
number of youthful symphonies and concertos to his credit. The

24

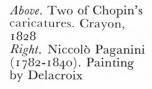

Above. Two of Chopin's caricatures. Crayon, 1828
Right. Niccolò Paganini (1782-1840). Painting by Delacroix

Overleaf. Berlin, Unter den Linden. Painting by Wilhelm Brücke, 1842

cosmopolitan atmosphere of Mendelssohn's world — Germany, Switzerland and France — did much to give him a confidence which Chopin lacked, and the famous Sunday morning concerts of the Mendelssohn family in Berlin helped publicise Mendelssohn's image and music in a way that Chopin might have envied.

The Berlin trip undoubtedly gave Chopin an anticipation of a more exciting and rewarding life. On returning to the confines of Warsaw in October he found the social life of the town, the balls and *soirées* and so on, very rural in outlook. He was easily bored, and within the year was off again on new travels and new adventures.

25

Academically, 1828 was spent in writing more exercises for the Conservatoire, but by now Chopin, an advanced student, sought to find a compromise between his own invention and the requirements of his professors. He composed a Piano Trio and dedicated it to Prince Antoine Radziwill, who had been so encouraging when Chopin played for the Tsar in 1825. He also wrote two more works for piano and orchestra: the Grand Fantasia on Polish Airs, and the beautiful and sensitive Krakoviak, a 'Grand Concert Rondo'. The *krakoviak* was a Polish national dance in duple metre, which originated in the Cracow region of southern Poland, in those days a republic separate from Warsaw, and a protectorate of Russia, Prussia and Austria. Unlike the mazurka and polonaise — which enjoyed wider popularity — the *krakoviak* influenced Chopin to a lesser extent. In this work, on the other hand, his development of dance motifs, and the lyrical poetry which blossoms from the opening mists of orchestral sound and the limpid piano phrases, is impressive in its evocation of atmosphere and colour, and the Krakoviak remains amongst the most carefully finished of Chopin's student works.

In the spring of 1829, during his last months at the Conservatoire, his family felt that nothing would be gained by keeping Chopin in Warsaw. On 13 April his father, relying on the impact of Chopin's reputation and future promise, sent a petition to the Minister of Public Relations, in which a request for funds was made in the interests of supporting Chopin on his intended travels through Europe, 'especially Germany, Italy and France, so as to form himself upon the best models'. Such a finishing course was normal for any young musicians of the period, and the custom lasted well into the present century. Officialdom, however, had little interest in reputation and promise: they maintained that if Chopin devoted his time to piano miniatures and showed no aptitude for academic subjects or set composition, there was almost certainly another student capable of such work and therefore more deserving of a grant. There were, of course, such students, but for all their study and appreciation of the rules, it is an ironic reflection that they faded into oblivion, their names not even preserved between the pages of history books.

During this time Nicholas I, Tsar of Russia in succession to Alexander I, was crowned King of Poland, and there was a polite, if bitter, reception from the Warsaw public. They had little to celebrate by the coronation of an invading ruler. Chopin's attention, predictably, was taken up by an event more immediate to his interests: the visit of Niccolò Paganini (23 May-19 July). Paganini's technical brilliance and 'devilish' mastery of the violin was at that time dazzling the musical life of Europe, and only a year earlier he had given concerts in Vienna which had taken that city, so critical in its judgement, by storm. Clothes appeared in shop windows described as 'in the style of Paganini', and the Emperor Franz I of Austria, one of the music loving members of the Habsburg family, created him 'Virtuoso of the Court'. Paganini's example exerted wide influence on 19th century musicians: Liszt, Schumann and Brahms were unanimous in their favourable reactions. Chopin, like Liszt, became aware of new potentials and new sonorities inherent in Paganini's example, and — typical of his desire to enshrine his youthful experiences in music — he soon afterwards wrote a little *Souvenir de Paganini*, based on the Italian air, *The Carnival of Venice*. The main effect of Paganini's influence emerged, however, in the first set of piano studies which Chopin began to sketch in the same autumn.

In the July Chopin took his final examinations in music. For all his waywardness and apparent disinterest in the curriculum, he passed without much difficulty. When he walked out of the doors of the Warsaw Conservatoire for the last time, his years of study behind him, he carried a glowing recommendation from Elsner, who drew attention in his report to Chopin's 'outstanding abilities [and] musical genius' — rare words from so formidable a teacher.

The young composer was now on his own, full of determination to make his way in an uncharitable world. The future was in his own hands.

Chapter 3

Travels and Farewell to Poland

'The native melody is like the climate of the mother country'—
Witwicki

Although Chopin's family had failed to obtain a grant from the
Minister, they were still no less insistent that he should go abroad,
despite their limited resources. He left Warsaw almost
immediately after his final examinations at the Conservatoire. His
destination was Vienna which, after Paris, was the most important
musical centre in Europe, though it no longer enjoyed the glories
of the 18th century rococo era. The atmosphere of Vienna still
reflected its heritage, however, and although numerous composers
penned **fashionable** *salon* music, the spirit of the great trio of
Haydn, Mozart and Beethoven loomed over everything.
Beethoven, indeed, had died only two years previously.

Journeying through Cracow, and climbing the passes of the
picturesque highlands of eastern Moravia, Chopin arrived in
Vienna on 31 July 1829. Within the week he had been to three
operas, but there was a more serious purpose to his visit. The
influential Austrian music publisher, Tobias Haslinger—whose
publications included some of the most important works of
Beethoven as well as some by Schubert— had already been sent
manuscripts of Chopin's First Piano Sonata, and the *Là ci darem*
Variations, but, a shrewd businessman, was reluctant to publish
music by a new and unknown composer. He changed his mind
after he had read a praiseworthy letter from Elsner, and had heard
Chopin play. He offered to publish the Variations—without
payment—on condition that Chopin play them at a public
concert. Chopin was unprepared for this. It was one thing to visit
Vienna on holiday and play privately, quite another to give a
concert under the critical ears of the Viennese public, particularly
when so much depended on the outcome. He was, as usual,
careless about his practice, and justifiably nervous, but the
enthusiasm of so many patrons of music in Vienna, the offer of a
fine Graf *Hammerflügel* to play, and the loan of a theatre, finally
persuaded him. On 11 August he gave his concert: 'I made my
entry into the world'. His main work, following a Beethoven

Tobias Haslinger
(1787-1842).
Watercolour by Joseph
Kriehuber, 1832
(Historisches Museum,
Vienna)

29

overture, was the *Là ci darem* Variations, which received a tumultuous reception. He also intended to introduce his Krakoviak but 'at rehearsals the orchestra accompanied so badly' that he was compelled to improvise. One of the themes he took was a Polish drinking song popular at weddings. This was *Chmiel,* among the oldest of folk polonaise tunes from western Poland. Chopin's paraphrase apparently 'electrified the public, as they are not used here to such songs. My spies in the stalls', he wrote home in a letter of 12 August, 'assure me that people even jumped on their seats!'

Despite such enthusiasm, the quiet reserve and delicacy of Chopin's playing does not seem to have been to the liking of the Viennese audience. The same letter continues: '. . . it is being said everywhere that I played too softly, or rather, too delicately for people used to the piano pounding of the artists here. I expect to find this reproach in the paper, especially as the editor's daughter thumps frightfully. It doesn't matter: there always must be a *but* somewhere, and I should rather it were that one than have people say I played too loudly'.

The impact of this first concert resulted nevertheless in another on 18 August. He wrote the day after: 'If I was well received the first time, it was still better yesterday. The moment I appeared on the stage there were bravos, repeated three times: and there was a larger audience. . . The second success was better than the first: it goes *crescendo,* that's what I like'. Among the works played was the Krakoviak, with the original rather weak orchestration now improved by Tomasz Nidecki, who had been a student at the Warsaw Conservatoire with Chopin, and who was now studying in Vienna.

Chopin became the attraction of the moment, a brilliant new star rising in the musical firmament. He met a number of influential people, including Czerny (who taught Liszt and had been a pupil of Beethoven) and Gyrowetz, a composer whose numerous works included concertos—one of which Chopin had played as a prodigy in Warsaw many years earlier—and over sixty symphonies. He was *Kapellmeister* to the Vienna Court, an important post. Chopin was also introduced to the Lichnowsky family, whose ancestral homeland was Poland. The family was among the best known of Viennese patrons and had been closely associated with Beethoven. Their most illustrious member, Prince Carl, had died in 1814, but Chopin met Count Moritz 'who couldn't praise me enough. . . He's the same who was Beethoven's greatest friend' (Beethoven had dedicated both his *Eroica* piano variations, Op. 35, and the E minor Piano Sonata to the Count).

Almost everybody, with the exception of the 'stony' Germans, complimented Chopin, yet he found that few musicians cared to accept him as a pupil. They frequently annoyed him with their surprise that anyone could learn so much in a provincial town like Warsaw: 'Under Zywny and Elsner the greatest donkey could learn', he would reply furiously.

A Viennese *Hammerflügel* by Conrad Graf, *c.* 1825. This particular piano was a gift to Beethoven and is now in the Beethoven-Haus, Bonn, where it was restored to playing condition in 1964

These petty irritations apart, Chopin's visit to Vienna was a success and he had made many new friends. On 19 August he left after 'tender farewells — really tender' for the next stage of his travels, Prague, the capital of the ancient king of Bohemia but in those days very much a part of the Austro-Hungarian empire under the rule of the Habsburg family. Like so many of the principal European centres, Prague had a great heritage of music going back a thousand years or more, and its audiences were amongst the most discriminating of the times. Their admiration, when roused, could be boundless — as in the case of Mozart's happy association with the city — but Chopin's visit was brief and uneventful, though he stayed long enough to observe, in a letter to his family dated Saturday 22 August, that 'the town is beautiful . . . when one sees it from the castle hill; large, ancient and once opulent'.

In spite of requests to give concerts, Chopin declined, mainly because he felt that his impression in Vienna was so favourable that the critical Prague public, who had casually dismissed

The Imperial Court Theatre by the Kärntnertor, the scene of the first performance of Beethoven's Ninth Symphony, and of Chopin's first concerts in Vienna. Engraving, anonymous, *c.* 1825.

Paganini, might do the same to him and so mar the reputation he was consolidating.

Leaving Prague he travelled by road through the Ore Mountains, making for the old city of Dresden. Surrounded by forests, with the Elbe flowing through the centre, Dresden was famous for its archietecture, art collections and libraries which had been greatly enriched during the reigns of the Electors of Saxony in the 17th and 18th centuries. To judge from the engravings and paintings of the period which have come down to us, it must have been a memorable sight in Chopin's day— resplendent churches, the tree-lined river spanned by delicately wrought bridges, and gondola-like ferries plying their trade or resting at anchor.

One highlight of the Dresden visit was a performance of Goethe's *Faust*. As a subject it had already attracted a good many composers. Beethoven once thought of using it as the basis for an opera, while Liszt was to write a symphony around the three main characters of the drama: Faust, the innocent Gretchen whose pure

Prague. Engraving, mid-19th century

33

Dresden. Engraving, *c.* 1807-08

spirit acts as a foil against Mephistopheles the Devil to whom Faust sells his soul in exchange for superhuman powers. The theme of *Faust* had first been set by Christopher Marlowe and was based on the actual exploits of a renaissance magician of renown, Johann (Georg) Faust, who had studied supernatural and black arts at the University of Cracow. Not surprisingly, he was held in some horror by God-fearing citizens, including Martin Luther.

The performance which Chopin attended on 28 August was one of the first dramatic realisations of Goethe's *magnum opus*. It had been completed some years earlier, but had only received its first staging a few months previously at Brunswick in Germany. Although the version Chopin heard was confined to Part I of the story, and was grossly mutilated, it did not fail to make an impression: 'I have just come back from *Faust*. I had to stand outside the theatre from half-past-four; the play lasted from six to eleven o'clock. . . It's a terrible phantasy but a great one. Between the acts they played selections from Spohr's opera of the same name'. Although Chopin was moved by the work, it is in character that he did not embrace the image of Faust or seek to emulate his example. There were many young men during the 19th century who identified themselves dangerously with the Faust legend, and, like Faust, lived to pay the price.

Vienna seen from the Belvedere. Painting by Canaletto

Leaving Dresden Chopin made for home, travelling through the Polish city of Breslau (now Wroclaw), the flat terrain of the land contrasting with the mountainous landscape of Bohemia and Saxony.

He arrived back in Warsaw on 12 September, and the remainder of that year (1829) was spent in evenings of music-making. On these occasions Chopin was not under the tremendous nervous strain of public concert giving, and could explore at ease the richly rewarding worlds of such works as Spohr's Octet and the *Archduke* Piano Trio, the C sharp minor String Quartet and the Opus 26 Piano Sonata of Beethoven, all of which left a deep and lasting impression. By now he was already enough of an artist to have developed discrimination and his regard for Beethoven shows this, for Beethoven's music had become increasingly unpopular with the Warsaw public. To some extent Chopin owed such admiration to the encouragement of Zywny, but in his own work he was still influenced to a degree by the example of such instantly successful and fashionable composers as Hummel, Moscheles and Kalkbrenner—musicians inferior, not only to the grandeur and stature of the Viennese school (with which they can hardly stand comparison), but to Chopin's own invention and poetry as well.

During these months Chopin began work on his most important

Johann Wolfgang
von Goethe (1749-1832).
Portrait in oils by Franz
Gerhard von Kügelgen,
c. 1808

composition to date, the Piano Concerto in F minor, completed the following spring. (This became known as No. 2 since it was published *after* the E minor Concerto we now know as No. 1.) It proved to be Chopin's first substantial work in which the inhibitions of his student years seem to have suddenly vanished. A new confidence had emerged.

The emotional character of the F minor Concerto and such smaller pieces as the *Lento con gran espressione* Nocturne — which used themes from the concerto — and in particular the poetic depth and the smouldering passions beneath the elegant, aristocratic veneer, was similarly indicative of a new mood. The turbulence of feeling offered a complete contrast with the simplicity and uninvolved attitude of previous works. Significantly, letters to his family remained somewhat reticent in language and content, but a different, more revealing approach is found in the correspondence with his old friend Titus Woyciechowski (to whom the *Là ci darem* Variations were dedicated). This shows Chopin to have been under considerable nervous stress. His plans to visit Berlin, Vienna and Italy did not materialise and though he could seek no extension of his art or fame in Warsaw, he remained attached to the town like a barnacle.

At long last he confessed in a letter of 3 October to Titus that he was deeply in love:

> .O, perhaps unfortunately, I already have my ideal, whom I have served faithfully, though silently, for half a year, of whom I dream, to thoughts of whom the *adagio* of my concerto [No. 2] belongs, and who this morning inspired the little waltz [Op. 70, No. 3, in D flat major] I am sending you ... You wouldn't believe how dreary I find Warsaw now. If it weren't for the family making it a little more cheerful, I wouldn't stay. But how dismal it is to have no one to go to in the morning to share one's griefs and joys; how hateful when something weighs on you and there's nowhere to lay it down. You know to what I refer. I often tell my pianoforte what I want to tell you.

Konstancja
Gladkowska (1810-89),
at the age of forty

The girl who had momentarily captured Chopin's youthful heart was a young and pretty Polish soprano, Konstancja Gladkowska, who was a few months younger than him. During her short career she became one of the best singers of her time, and like Chopin had enrolled at the Warsaw Conservatoire, where they met, in 1826, But Konstancja had many admirers, especially the young cavalry officers attached to the local garrison. In their dashingly-cut uniforms, ready to fight a duel to the death to protect her honour, they offered a hopelessly one-sided competition for Chopin, who found it difficult to develop a friendship and sought, fatally, to idealise Konstancja at a distance.

Chopin's father probably knew little of his son's plight but was certainly annoyed and frustrated by his listless outlook on life. He took matters into his own hands and at the end of October sent Chopin to visit Prince Antoine Radziwill at his country estate. This diversion put Konstancja out of Chopin's thoughts, at least on the surface. He was attracted to the Prince's two young daughters and wrote to Titus on 14 November: 'So far as my temporary personal pleasure went, I would have stopped there [at the Radziwill castle] till they turned me out, but my affairs, particularly my unfinished concerto, which is waiting impatiently for the completion of the finale, spurred me on to abandon that paradise. There were two Eves in it: young princesses, very kind and friendly, musical, sensitive creatures'. He gave a few lessons to one of them, Wanda: 'She is quite young: seventeen and pretty; really it was a joy to guide her little fingers'.

(Prince Radziwill incidentally was a composer and cellist, and greatly impressed Chopin when he showed him the manuscript of an opera he had written on the Faust theme. Chopin was so impressed, in fact, that when writing to Titus he felt compelled to discuss some of the work's technical and theatrical details, something he only rarely did since he felt that music needed neither descriptive nor programmatic help. He always felt that it was an art form which made its most immediate emotional and intellectual impact through the medium of performance, a conventional attitude but no less valid for that.)

Back in Warsaw, with winter fast approaching, Chopin continued work on the F minor Concerto, his feelings for Konstancja were re-kindled, and he began to take heed of the demands of Warsaw audiences. He had already given two successful concerts in Vienna, and the Warsaw newspapers voiced the mood of the people when they wrote: 'Does not Mr. Chopin's talent belong to his country? Does he think that Poland is incapable of appreciating him? Mr. Chopin's works bear unquestionably the stamp of genius'. He found he could delay his first major appearance in Warsaw no longer, and so on 3 March 1830 a trial concert was arranged in the drawing room of the Chopin household, with a select private audience. The Polish composer, Kurpiński, who with Elsner was manager of the Warsaw Opera and was the composer of some twenty-four Italianate operas, conducted, and Chopin played his Fantasia on Polish Airs (which included one of Kurpiński's own melodies) and the completed F minor Concerto. It was a success and on 17 March Chopin made his official adult *début* at the National Theatre in Warsaw, playing the same works.

The concert was sold out three days beforehand, and the audience was full of admiration. One of them, moved by the experience and oblivious of time — eleven o'clock at night — wrote enthusiastically:

I have just returned from the concert by Chopin, that artist whom I heard playing when he was seven, when he was still a hope for the future. How beautifully he plays today! What fluency! What evenness! . . . his music is full of expressive feeling and song, and puts the listener into a state of subtle rapture, bringing back to his memory all the happy moments he has known.

38

Chopin was not satisfied, however, and felt that his real success came with a second concert, given a few days later on the 22nd in response to public demand. On this occasion he offered the Krakoviak in place of the Fantasia, and used a more powerfully toned Viennese piano which projected the sound further than his own quiet instrument.

In the meantime Haslinger in Vienna kept his promise and in January had published the *Là ci darem* Variations. This did much to promote Chopin's name among Austrian and German musicians. Come April he began work on the E minor Piano Concerto (known as No. 1). This is arguably a work less delicate and less emotional in style than the F minor but the shadow of Konstancja still haunts the slow movement: 'It is not meant to be loud — it's more of a romance, quiet, melancholy; it should give the impression of gazing tenderly at a place which brings to mind a thousand dear memories. It is a sort of meditation in beautiful spring weather but by moonlight' (letter to Titus, 15 May).

The summer months were spent in completing the new work and, as always, attending the opera whenever he could. During the Tsar's opening of the Polish Diet (Parliament) in May and June, a host of brilliant artists visited Warsaw and Chopin was full of praise for them, especially for the famous German Henrietta Sontag, the original soprano of Beethoven's Ninth and the *Missa Solemnis*. On 24 July he attended Konstancja's concert *début*. His old feelings for her were soon awakened, but by now he was sufficiently over the worse period to view her singing critically and without the blind adoration one might have expected.

In August the Chopin family went to their old home at Zelazowa Wola, but by September Chopin was already planning to leave Poland for new travels and successes. The unsettled political climate in Europe at that time, however, altered many of his plans. On the 22nd he wrote to Titus:

> My father did not wish me to travel, a few weeks ago, on account of the disturbances which are starting all over Germany: not counting the Rhine provinces, the Saxons – who already have another king— Brunswick, Cassel, Darmstadt and so on. We heard, too, that in Vienna some thousands of people had begun to become sulky about the flour. I don't know what was wrong with the flour, but I know there was something. In the Tyrol, also, there have been arguments. The Italians do nothing but boil over . . . I have not yet tried for my passport, but people tell me that I can get one only to Austria and Prussia; no use to think of Italy and France. And I know that several persons have been refused passports altogether, but that would doubtless not happen to me. So I shall probably go within the next few weeks through Cracow to Vienna, for people there have now refreshed their memory of me [i.e. the publication of the Variations] and I must take advantage of that.

During these weeks he completed the E minor Concerto, and gave the first public performance of it on 11 October 1829 at the Town Hall, at what proved to be his final concert in Warsaw. The concerto was the centrepiece of the programme, together with the Fantasia on Polish Airs, and the concert was an overwhelming success: 'I was not a bit, not a bit nervous', he wrote to Titus the day after, 'and played the way I play when I'm alone, and it went well'. There was, too, an element of personal satisfaction, for Konstancja also took part, 'dressed in white, with roses in her hair'. By now the two had got to know each other, but although he still felt well disposed towards her, she clearly had never felt the same emotions for him. Later in her life, after Chopin's death, she was surprised to read of his love for her: all she could say was that 'he was temperamental, full of fantasies, and unreliable'.

In spite of Chopin's fatalistic premonition that 'when I leave it will be to forget home for ever: I feel that I am leaving home only to die', the fateful day for departure had to be chosen. He left Warsaw, his family and Konstancja — with whom he exchanged rings — on 2 November 1830.

Childhood had become a thing of the past, and Chopin stood on the threshold of his future, a brilliant pianist and composer. On the outskirts of Warsaw, Elsner conducted a special little cantata he had written for the occasion: the coach made its way towards Vienna, and Chopin, in a sense tracing in reverse the very footsteps of his father before him, left his homeland and prepared to face the harsh reality of life on the troubled stage of Europe.

Chapter 4

New Horizons

'His inspirations were powerful, fantastic, impulsive'—Liszt

Chopin's original plans for his journey to Vienna were altered, and the route he finally took, with Titus as companion, was the same as that taken on his return to Warsaw from Vienna the previous year.

In Breslau he played two movements of the E minor Concerto at a private gathering: one diverting outcome of this centred around a local amateur pianist who, after he had heard Chopin play, hurriedly backed out of his own commitments to perform.

The next stop was Dresden, where Chopin renewed his friendship with the German composer, August Klengel, a former pupil of Clementi and official organist to the Dresden Court. Chopin had first met Klengel in Prague in 1829 and liked him: 'I respect him greatly... I like to talk with him because one can really learn something'. Klengel tried to persuade Chopin to give a concert, 'but about that I am deaf. I have no time to lose, and Dresden will give me neither fame nor money' (letter to his family, 14 November). Nevertheless he played one of his concertos for Klengel privately: 'It reminded him of Field's playing, that I have a rare touch, that although he had heard much about me, he had never expected to find me such a virtuoso. It was not idle compliment: he told me that he hates to flatter anyone or force himself to praise them' (21 November).

After passing through Prague, Chopin and Titus arrived in Vienna on 22 November. If his earlier visit to the city had been both encouraging and flattering, Chopin this time encountered a cool reserve when it came to the question of giving concerts or promoting his music. On a social level he was still made welcome, but social niceties hardly helped his funds. Haslinger politely refused to publish his music; no doubt he had made a loss on the *Là ci darem* Variations, for in those days Viennese audiences, taking their cue from the example of the Habsburg monarchy, preferred the waltzes of the Strauss family or Joseph Lanner, and had an insatiable appetite for fantasias and trite pot-pourries on popular operatic tunes. Chopin observed to Elsner that 'here waltzes are called works!', while in an earlier letter he remarked on 'the

Chopin.
Watercolour, anonymous
c. 1830

43

The Paradeplatz in Vienna, a popular walking spot. Engraving by Leopold Beyer, 1805

corrupt taste of the Viennese public'. Commercialism rather than artistic integrity dictated the policy of many Austrian music publishers, and they had little time for the poetic sensitivity or originality of Chopin's music.

Neither was the delicate, unspectacular quality of his piano playing a commercial proposition. One concert impressario told Chopin that he could not advise him to become a soloist 'for there are so many good pianists here that one needs a great reputation to gain anything'.

In letters home Chopin made a pretence of enjoying himself for no doubt he did not wish to worry his family. He attended *soirées* and lavish balls given by the nobility and, with Titus, found lodgings in one of the main streets of Vienna, the Kohlmarkt: 'three rooms, on the third floor, it's true, but delightful, splendid, elegantly furnished'. By day the street bustled noisily with people and the cobblestones rang with the sound of horses' hooves and the rattle of carriages. By night the tall houses—with their long

44

A masked ball in the
Redoutensaal, the
Hofburg, Vienna.
Engraving by J. Schütz,
c. 1800 (Hans
Swarowsky Collection)

windows and carved masonry over silent shops — were illuminated
by solitary gas lamps, becoming a shadowy world of fantasy and
fairy tale.

On the Wednesday before Christmas (22 December) Chopin
wrote home saying that he now had rooms on the *fourth* floor:
'How nice it is. . . A roof opposite me and pigmies down below. I
am higher than they! The best moment is when, having finished
playing on Graf's dull piano, I go to bed with your letters in my
hand. Then, even in sleep, I see only you! . . . I don't want to say
goodbye to you, I should like to keep on writing'. He allows just a
little of his anxiety to mar the cheerful pose: 'In one way I am glad
to be here, but in another!'

A completely different Chopin — depressed, lonely, and
uncertain of his future — emerges in letters to his friends,
particularly to Jan Matuszyński, to whom he unburdened his
frustrations freely. His mood reached a point of feverish,
melancholic despondency with the news that Warsaw had revolted

against the Russians. He feared Russian reprisals and worried about his family and his home, about everything he had ever known and loved.

The revolt was yet another disturbance in a Europe seething with discontent, each country anxious to assert its national identity and to be free from the yoke of foreign overlords. It stemmed more immediately from reports—which soon reached Poland—of the Paris revolution in the July of that year. Discontented army factions at once planned an overthrow of the Russian dominated government, choosing a moment when Russia was already engaged in a war with the Ottoman Empire. But the attempt was abortive and it was not until November, a few weeks after Chopin left Warsaw, that the Polish army found itself strong enough to mount an uprising, which Titus joined as soon as he heard the news in Vienna, leaving a worried Chopin behind. Bad leadership, however, led to confusion, distrust and much suffering. A 'National Revolution' was declared at a meeting of the Diet on 18 December 1830, and by the 21st the situation was explosive. The Russians declared the Polish act of defiance to be an 'odious

The Kohlmarkt, Vienna. Engraving by Beyer

46

St. Stephen's
Cathedral, Vienna.
Tinted copper plate by
by Vincenz Reim
(Historisches Museum,
Vienna)

crime' and an army, 120,000 strong, marched towards Lithuania
to crush the usurpers of power.

   On Christmas day Chopin wrote a long letter to Jan, a letter
which was by then full of familiar turbulent changes of
mood — from the depths of depression to carefree comments on his
surroundings. Vienna was a city suddenly hostile towards the
Poles — Austria, in fact, maintained a neutral stand in the
Russo-Polish conflict — and Chopin found himself a lone wolf,
with few compensations. It was his first Christmas away from his
family, and his letter to Jan opens with a wistful contradiction of
the traditional Christmas spirit:

Today I am sitting alone, in a dressing-gown, gnawing my ring and writing. If it were not that I should be a burden on my father, I would come back. I curse the day I left. I am up to the neck in evening parties, concerts and dances, but they bore me to death; everything is so terribly gloomy and depressing for me here. I have to dress and get ready to go out: in company I must appear calm, and then when I come home I let myself go on the piano. The other part [of your letter] has grieved me deeply. Is there really not even a little change? Did she [Konstancja] not fall ill? I could easily believe such thing about so sensitive a creature. . . Is it perhaps the terror of the 29th [of November, the actual day of the revolt]? May God forbid that it should be my fault! Calm her, say that so long as my strength lasts—that till death—that even after death, my ashes will strew themselves at her feet.

Later he describes Midnight Service in the cathedral of St. Stephen which was in the centre of the walled city of Vienna, and overlooked the gently curving waters of the Danube flowing eastwards towards the Black Sea in the eye of the rising sun:

When I entered there was no one there. Not to hear the Mass, but just to look at the huge building at that hour. I got into the darkest corner at the foot of a Gothic pillar. I can't describe the greatness, the magnificence of those huge arches. It was quiet; now and then the footsteps of a sacristan, lighting candles at the back of the sanctuary, would break into my lethargy. A coffin behind me, a coffin under me—only the coffin above me was lacking . . . I have never felt my loneliness so clearly.

A few paragraphs later he asks:

Shall I go to Paris? The people here advise me to wait. Shall I come back to Poland? Shall I stay here? Shall I put an end to myself? Shall I stop writing to you? Advise me what to do.

He spent several days writing this letter and towards the end his gloom had worn off somewhat, and he gives a pen sketch of his daily routine:

My room is big and comfortable, with three windows, the bed opposite the windows; a splendid pantaleon* on the right side, a sofa on the left, mirrors between the windows; in the middle, a fine, big, round mahogany table; a polished parquet floor. It's quiet . . . so I can concentrate my thoughts on all of you. In the morning I am called by an insufferably stupid servant. I get up, they bring me coffee; I play and mostly have a cold breakfast. About 9 comes the *maitre* for the German language. After that I usually play . . . all this in a dressing-gown until noon. After that comes a very worthy German . . . who works in the prison, and if the weather is fine we go for a walk on the *glacis* round the town, after which I go to dinner if I am invited anywhere. If not we go together to the place frequented by the entire academic youth: that is Zur Boemische Köchlin. After dinner, black coffee is drunk in the best *kaffeehaus*—that is the custom here. Then I pay visits, return home at dusk, curl my hair, change my shoes, and go out for the evening; about 10, 11 or sometimes 12—never later—I come back, play, weep, look, laugh, go to bed, put the light out, and always dream about some of you.

*By the end of the 18th century a term virtually synonymous with 'piano'.

But such lightness of spirit was short-lived. Only a few days later, on 1 January 1831, he wrote another letter to Jan, and his powerful narrative again evoked an atmosphere of despair. We can almost relive with Chopin this crucial period in which the division between childhood and family love and protection and the responsibilities and ultimate isolation of manhood was so relentless and abrupt:

> What are my friends doing? I live with you all, I would die for you, for all of you. Why am I so alone? Is it only you who can be together at so fearful a moment? . . . Today is New Year—how sadly I begin it! Perhaps I shall not end it. Embrace me. You are going to the war. Come back a colonel. Good luck to you all. Why can't I beat the drum!

Youthful reveries seem suddenly to have become part of a very remote past. Chopin could not reconcile himself to the inevitability of his fate.

During this period of emotional stress, it is hardly surprising that he felt unable to devote much serious thought to composition, or to furthering his career as a pianist. He drafted sketches for the Grande Polonaise, Op. 22, for piano and orchestra, and wrote the Grande Valse Brillante, Op. 18, both to some extent gestures to attract the dance-loving Viennese public. Even so he found it impossible to provide them with conventional dances, and although the music of that time reflects a youthful exuberance for virtuosity, it is also rather impersonal in style, as if Chopin cared little for what he wrote.

Far more characteristic of his impassioned feelings were two works written between the May and June of 1831 and perfected some time later: the hectic First Scherzo—in which he introduced a Polish Christmas song veiled in the surrounding harmonies of the central section—and the dramatic First Ballade, a form and concept he was to make especially his own. During the 19th century, in an age when it was more fashionable than now to nickname favourite pieces, someone labelled this the *Polish* Ballade. Schumann described it as among Chopin's 'wildest and most original compositons' and in one of his letters to Heinrich Dorn he wrote that Chopin thought it the best of his own works. Today it still enjoys the enormous popularity of years ago. The folk song used in the Scherzo was one of the few instances in Chopin's music where he resorted to such *direct* quotation. The melody, *Lullaby, little Jesus,* is still known to Polish peasants today, and the English composer, Alan Rawsthorne, once recalled how he 'heard a Polish peasant singing this tune, high up in the Tatra Mountains. The effect was strangely moving in the stillness of the craggy rocks with their patches of snow. His voice came from nowhere in particular, ventriloquially, floating through the mountain air. He sang with abandon, in a quite uninhibited fashion, and with a certain hard, almost ruthless quality that enables the Slavs to get to the heart of their most poignant melodies'.*

Homesickness and thoughts of his childhood friends on the battle fields of Poland, thoughts which so perpetually haunted Chopin, stimulated, too, a number of settings of poems by Polish nationalist poets including Stefan Witwicki. The following lines from Witwicki's *The Sad Stream,* set by Chopin at this time, seem a particularly vivid reflection of Chopin's mood; one can almost see him staring at the Danube, far from his home, from Warsaw and the Vistula, and musing in sorrow and nostalgic memory:

> River from foreign regions,
> why is your current so murky?
> Has the bank fallen in somewhere,
> have old snows melted?
>
> The old snows lie on the mountains,
> flowers bloom on my banks,
> but there, by my spring,
> a mother weeps at my spring.
>
> Seven daughters she has brought up,
> seven daughters she has buried,
> seven daughters in the middle of the garden,
> with their heads facing the east.
>
> Now she greets their ghosts,
> she asks the children about their comfort,
> and the waters their graves
> and sings pitiful songs.

Stefan Witwicki (1800-47). Medallion in bronze by Wladyslaw Oleszczyński

(Stefan Witwicki — 1800-47 — was a close friend of Chopin, and in Paris enjoyed a friendship with Mickiewicz until political differences caused a rift between the two men.)

Eventually Chopin managed to pull himself together. Living in a world of memories and emotions of the past was no substitute for creating a new life in the present. He mustered enough strength and will-power to give a concert on 4 April, at the famous Redoutensaal, but it was not a success. Billed simply as 'Herr Chopin (piano player)', he offered as a solo item his E minor Concerto — such arrangements were popular at the time — and was one of ten artists taking part. He made little impact and found himself unable to recapture a moment of his earlier glories in Vienna. Just two days before the concert Chopin jotted some rambling thoughts in his notebook which show how much he was out of his element during these months:

> Today it was beautiful on the Prater. Crowds of people with whom I have nothing to do. I admired the foliage, the spring smell, and that innocence of nature which brought back my childhood's feelings. A storm was threatening, so I went indoors—but there was no storm. Only I got melancholy; why? I don't care for even music

*Alan Walker (ed.) *Frédéric Chopin: Profiles of the Man and the Musician* (London 1966).

today. It's late but I'm not sleepy: I don't know what is wrong with me... The newspapers and posters have announced my concert. It's to be in two day's time but it is as if there was no such thing: it doesn't seem to concern me. I don't listen to the compliments; they seem to me stupider and stupider. I wish I were dead and yet I would like to see my parents. Her [Konstancja's] image stands before my eyes: I think I don't love her any more, and yet I can't get her out of my head. Everything I have seen abroad till now seems to me old and hateful and just makes me sigh for home, for those blessed moments that I didn't know how to value. What used to seem great, today seems common; what I used to think common is now incomparable, too great, too high. The people here are not my people: they're kind, but kind from habit; they do everything too respectably, flatly, moderately. I don't even want to think of moderation. I'm puzzled, I'm melancholy, I don't know what to do with myself. I wish I were not alone . . .

The failure of his visit to Vienna, his unhappiness, the irritating superficial charms of his hosts, and the lack of recognition — all these finally decided him to leave the city and make for new horizons. He began to make plans for his departure at the end of June. He wanted to go to Paris, but as he was legally of Russian nationality this presented difficulties, for Paris then was a refuge for Polish revolutionaries and exiles domiciled in France and plotting subversive activities against the Russians. Finally he secured a passport to London, with the important proviso 'passing through Paris'. That was sufficient.

He travelled west along the valley of the Danube to the north of the picturesque Austrian Tyrol, passing first through Salzburg, Mozart's birthplace, and then on to Munich. Here he stopped longer than intended, for money due from his father had not arrived and communications with Warsaw were practically at a standstill. He took what opportunity this delay offered, and gave a very successful concert on 28 August in the Philharmonic Society Hall. The programme included the Fantasia on Polish Airs and the E minor Concerto. It was the first success he had had since leaving Warsaw.

But a week later, having arrived in Stuttgart, his temporary elation was shattered with the news of Warsaw's downfall on 7-8 September. Since the November revolution, tension in Warsaw had, of course, greatly increased. In a brave effort to assert their independence, the Poles had declared themselves a free state with no ties to the Tsar; this was in January. The Russians carried out their threats and Nicholas I sent a fresh army of 200,000 men against a mere 40,000 Polish nationalists who finally sought refuge in Warsaw for their last stand. As so often happens in such situations, no one really cared enough to support the Polish cause and engage in a war with the might of Russia. The besieged city panicked, riots broke out, cholera became rampant, and the people fought for their lives and liberty. At the mercy of the guns they were eventually forced to surrender, and their loss of even the partial independence they enjoyed before was completed six

51

Stuttgart. Drawing
by Antoine Richard,
Illustrirte Zeitung, 1847

months later, in February 1832, when Poland became a province
of the Russian Empire. They were not to know independence again
until the present century, and then only for a brief period between
the two world wars.

The news left Chopin in a state of utter despair. In his notebook
he left frantic, almost incoherent fragments:

> The suburbs are destroyed, burned. Jaś, Wiluś probably dead in the
> trenches. I see Marcel a prisoner! That good fellow Sowiński in the
> hands of those brutes! Paszkiewicz! Some dog from Mohilov holds
> the seat of the first monarchs of Europe. Moscow rules the world!
> O God, do you exist? You're there and You don't avenge it. How
> many more Russian crimes do You want—or—or are You a Russian
> too!!? My poor Father! The dear old man may be starving, my
> mother not able to buy bread? Perhaps my sisters have succumbed
> to the ferocity of Muscovite soldiery let loose? Oh Father, what a
> comfort for your old age! Mother! Poor suffering Mother, have you
> borne a daughter to see a Russian violate her very bones! Mockery!
> Has even her [Emilia's] grave been respected? Trampled, thousands
> of other corpses are over the grave. What has happened to her
> [Konstancja]? Where is she? Poor girl, perhaps in some Russian's
> hands—a Russian strangling her, killing, murdering! Ah my Life,
> I'm here alone; come to me, I'll wipe away your tears, I'll heal the
> wounds of the present, remind you of the past—the days when there
> were no Russians, the days when the only Russians were a few who
> were very anxious to please you, and you were laughing at them
> because I was there. Have you your mother? Such a cruel mother,
> and mine is so kind. But perhaps I have no mother, perhaps some
> Russian has killed her, murdered. My sisters, raving, resist—father
> in despair, nothing he can do—and I here, useless! And I here with
> empty hands! Sometimes I can only groan, and suffer, and pour out
> my despair at the piano! God, shake the earth, let it swallow up the

men of this age, let the heaviest chastisement fall on France, that would not come to help us—

—The bed I go to—perhaps corpses have lain on it, lain long—yet today that does not sicken me. Is a corpse any worse than I? A corpse knows nothing of father, of mother, of sisters, of Titus; a corpse has no beloved, its tongue can hold no conversation with those who surround it—a corpse is as colourless as I, as cold as I am cold to everything now—

—The clocks in the towers of Stuttgart strike the hours of the night. How many new corpses is this minute making in the world? Mothers losing children, children losing mothers. So much grief over the dead, and so much delight! A vile corpse and a decent one—virtues and vice are all one, they are sisters when they are corpses. Evidently, then, death is the best act of man. And what is the worst? Birth: it is direct opposition to the best thing. I am right to be angry that I came into the world. What use is my existence to anyone? I am not fit for human beings, for I have neither snout nor calves to my legs; and does a corpse have them? A corpse also has no calves, so it lacks nothing of a mathematical fraternity with death. Did she [Konstancja] love me, or was she only pretending?

The Warsaw
Uprising. Lithograph by
Nicolas-Eustace Maurin

That's a knotty point to get over—Yes, no, yes, no, no, yes—finger by finger—Does she love me? Surely she loves me, let her do what she likes—

—Father! Mother! Where are you? Corpses? Perhaps some Russian has played tricks—oh wait—wait—But tears—they have not flowed for so long—oh, so long, so long I could not weep—how glad—how wretched—Glad and wretched—If I'm wretched, I can't be glad—and yet it is sweet—This is a strange state—but that is so with a corpse; it's well and not well with it at the same moment. It is transferred to a happier life and is glad, it regrets the life it is leaving and is sad. It must feel as I felt when I left off weeping. It was like some momentary death of feeling; for a moment I died in my heart; no, my heart died in me for a moment. Ah, why not for always! Perhaps it would be more endurable then. Alone! Alone! There are no words for my misery; how can I bear this feeling—

It was about this time that Chopin wrote his C minor Study which closes his first set of twelve piano Studies, Op. 10. Legend has it that this most famous of pieces was directly inspired by Warsaw's downfall, and it became known as the *Revolutionary* Study—one man's symbol of storm and tragedy. It is difficult today to confirm this story—during the 19th century many writers

General view of Paris. Woodcut by Jean-Jacques Champin, *L'Illustration*, 1852

wove fanciful tales around Chopin's works, encouraged by the unquestioning idealisation of Liszt's biography — but it is still widely recalled. Although it may have little origins in truth, its associations, even for the Poles themselves, are still vivid. The rushing, torrent-like cascades of sound, and the dramatic, rhetorical melody pausing for moments of lyrical repose, then surging forth with renewed passion, seems to eloquently sum up the feelings and innermost thoughts of a troubled Chopin.

After the initial reaction, Chopin pulled himself together and set out for Paris. He arrived in mid-September and was destined to spend the remaining and most important years of his life in this most cosmopolitan of cities. Living as a self-enforced exile — though with no interest in the political agitations of his compatriots — he had in a sense returned to the land of his forefathers, the land *his* father had forsaken so many decades earlier. Chopin did not know this: a strain of Polish blood flowed through his veins and the imagery of Poland had shaped his youth. The heritage and splendour of that country, .her past musical glories — all became stylised in a strange, timeless pageant under Chopin's hands. The Poland he once knew was far away, perhaps gone forever. A moment of it was immortalised in his music. His heart and imagination forged a spirit of arrogant resistance, an endless tone-poem embodying the soul, mood and nationalism of a repressed people.

In Paris he found the atmosphere he needed. It became the stage on which his greatest triumphs were to be acted.

Chapter 5

Paris I

'Paris is whatever you choose'—Chopin

For nearly half a century before Chopin reached Paris, France had been the centre of both turmoil and reform. Napoleon, needless to say, was the oustanding figure of the period. He forged a new country, occupied Europe, and won himself a place in history. The most significant long term result of his rule in France was the establishment of a modern administrative system for the country, and the emergence of new liberties for the common majority of the land, rights previously controlled by the nobility who cared little

The execution of Louis XVI (1754-93). German engraving, anonymous (Carnavalet Museum, Paris)

Marie Antoinette
(1755-93). Portrait by
Madame Vige-Lebrun

for the lot of the peasant population. Deprived of their freedom
to express themselves, the mass had originally risen against the
King, Louis XVI, and his queen, Marie Antoinette, in the
storming of the Bastille — that prison which so symbolised royal
tyranny — in July 1789. Their grievances were justified. How, after
all, could a nation be governed by a feeble king who sought only to
satisfy his own pleasures — hunting, eating, mending clocks and
sleeping in the council chamber of his lavish palace at
Versailles — and a queen who felt compelled in the national
interest to retain just 500 servants and to buy only four new pairs of
shoes a week?

The 1789 revolution led to some reform, but extremists like
Robespierre were anxious to overthrow the king altogether.
Eventually they won the day and in 1793 Louis was guillotined and
the First Republic declared. From chaos order emerged when the
excesses of the revolution and the resultant suffering finally

ended. New reforms were introduced, the rights of the aristocracy withdrawn, the lot of the peasants improved, and slavery abolished.

The meteoric rise of Napoleon Bonaparte, a young Corsican general, was the consecration of the First Republic. He was elected Consul in 1799, but the public voted that he should be proclaimed Emperor, and in 1804 he was duly crowned, an action which aroused much critical judgement. Originally a champion of *liberty*, Napoleon had, in effect, revoked the ideals of the revolution; he was now a dictator and his rule was absolute — from army orders to artistic comment. All the same, his strong leadership did bring stability to an unbalanced France, as well as prosperity and security to a nation which had long forgotten the meaning of such virtues.

But dreams of military power and conquest haunted Napoleon, and were ultimately his ruination. He faced defeat at Trafalgar in 1805 and his supremacy began to be questioned. The final test of his claims came in 1812 with the invasion of Russia. Count Philippe-Paul de Ségur, one of his generals and aides-de-camp, went on this ill fated campaign and in 1824 published a stirring account of its hopes and tragedies.* In the July of 1812 he wrote, 'the Russian frontier stretched before us. Through the gloom our eager eyes strained to see into this glorious promised land. We imagined we heard the joyful shouts of the Lithuanians at the approach of their deliverers... We would be surrounded by love and gratitude'. In August Napoleon's armies captured Smolensk on their way to Moscow: 'We passed through the smoking ruins in military formation, with our martial music and customary pomp, triumphant over this desolation, but with no other witness to our glory'. In September Moscow was reached, but Napoleon had miscalculated the onslaught of the bitter Russian winter. Victory turned to defeat as his men retreated. Like hunted animals the Grand Army fled and collapsed slowly: 'This army had numbered one hundred thousand combatants on leaving Moscow. In twenty-five days it had been reduced to thirty-six thousand!... The silence was broken only by the crack of whips applied to horses... we dropped into hollows and had to climb back up the icy slopes, with men, horses and cannon rolling over each other in the darkness'.

For Napoleon this was the end, save for a last desperate stand by a morally and physically weakened Old Guard at the battle of Waterloo in 1815, who were defeated by the combined British and Prussian armies. With Napoleon's official abdication in 1814, the Congress of Vienna defined the limits of France and re-organised the structure of an occupied Europe. Louis XVIII, long since recognised as the official king of France by the *emigrée* French, came to the throne.

Napoleon's Russian Campaign, trans. J. David Townsend (London 1959) from *Histoire de Napoléon et de la Grande Armée pendant l'année 1812*.

Napoleon Bonaparte
(1769-1821). Detail from
a portrait by Anne
Louis Girodet-Troison
(Arenenberg Castle,
Switzerland)

Louis XVIII was an undistinguished monarch, though in the beginning he endeavoured to continue the political reforms of Napoleon's era. He was, however, a weak man and more outspoken forces soon came into force under his brother, later Charles X. Charles was only interested in carrying on the tradition of pre-revolutionary France. He had spent his exile at the Palace of Holyrood, in Scotland, where he is said to have worn a different pair of jewelled shoe-buckles on each day of the year. He reduced civil liberties and chose formerly influential aristocrats as his advisers; he also imposed a press censor and dismissed parliament. He had little interest in the affairs of the ordinary public.

Such a state could not last. The spirit of the 1789 Revolution had been epoch making, and the Russian defeat of Napoleon had spurred numerous countries to seek their freedom. Could the people of France, the seed from which the ideal of liberty had sprung, remain silent and unprotesting? Elements of unrest once again reached a climax in July 1830, when Paris became another scene of revolution: Charles X was overthrown and Louis Philippe, an opponent of the royalist régime and a supporter of democracy, was placed on the throne. Known as the 'citizen king' he was Duke of Orleans, and his reign became known as the 'July Monarchy'. Although he had good intentions it can be said that he never came to grips with the problems which faced his people.

Boulevard Poissonière
Paris. Painting by
Isidore Dagnan
(Carnavalet Museum)

The young Paris intellectuals of the day formed themselves into a group called 'Children of the Century'. Their philosophy embodied the politically orientated example of Robespierre and Danton, and they advocated freedom of speech and thought. They cared little for the formalised tradition and restrictive etiquette of their immediate past, seeking instead a new language of expression. Of course, as in any momentous period, the fanatics tended to carry things too far, but the most perceptive artists,

Honoré de Balzac
(1799-1850). Etching by
Pierre-Edmond-
Alexandre Hédouin

writers and musicians voiced new emotions and dramatic tensions
in a way that showed a subtle awareness of both their time and
their classical heritage.

Chopin found himself suddenly plunged into this group and
though their values and ideals as we shall see, were basically
contrary to his own, for the moment they formed the core of one of
the most outstanding and colourful gatherings ever to congregate
and influence one another at the same place and the same moment

61

of time. Victor Hugo, Balzac and Lamartine formed the literary spearhead, while Delacroix led the romantic school of painters. It was Delacroix who left a vivid account of his total pre-occupation with the artistic and intellectual problems of the day, and in 1838 painted one of the most distinctive portraits of Chopin (now in the Louvre Musuem) which shows the gaunt, haunted planes of the face that typified Chopin in his later years. Among the musicians the most progressive were Liszt, eighteen months younger than Chopin, and Berlioz, whose astonishingly bold and brilliantly conceived *Fantastic* Symphony — one of the first dramatic breaks with the classicism of the Beethoven period — had been performed in Paris less than a year before Chopin's arrival.

At first the atmosphere and impact of Paris overwhelmed Chopin, but before long he had settled down and his letters assumed a calmer outlook on life. He seems to have learnt to control his anxieties, and we seldom find again in his

FRIED KALKBRENNER

Friedrich
Kalkbrenner
(1785-1849). Steel
engraving by Mayer

correspondence those same, uninhibited displays of emotion which characterised the months between leaving Warsaw and coming to Paris.

His first Paris home — comfortable but expensive — was on the fifth floor of No. 27 Boulevard Poissonière, a spacious, tree-lined avenue: 'A delightful lodging; I have a little room beautifully furnished with mahogany, and a balcony over the boulevard from which I can see from Montmartre to the Pantheon and the whole length of the fashionable quarter; many people envy my view, though not my stairs!' (18 November 1831).

The spirit of Paris is reflected in his correspondence: 'Paris is whatever you choose', he wrote to Titus in December. 'You can amuse yourself, be bored, laugh, cry, do anything you like, and nobody looks at you, and everyone goes his own way. I don't know where there can be so many pianists as in Paris. . .'

In the meantime he had brought with him several useful letters of introduction from influential people in Vienna. One was to Ferdinand Paer, among the most prominent musicians of the day, and conductor of the Court Theatre in Paris; earlier he had been associated with the Italian Opéra. As court musician to Napoleon he accompanied him to Warsaw in 1806 (when the city was liberated from Prussian rule, only to be subsequently created a Grand Duchy under another foreign king, this time Frederick Augustos I of Saxony). Paer readily introduced Chopin to the most illustrious figures in the musical world, including Rossini, Kalkbrenner and the veteran, Cherubini. Kalkbrenner made perhaps the greatest impression on the young composer who voiced his unbound admiration in a letter to Titus of 12 December:

You would not believe how curious I was about Herz, Liszt, Hiller and so on. They are all zero besides Kalkbrenner. I confess that I have played like Herz, but would wish to play like Kalkbrenner. If Paganini is perfection, Kalkbrenner is his equal but in quite another style. It is hard to describe to you his calm, his enchanting touch, his incomparable evenness, and the mastery that is displayed in every note; he is a giant walking over Herz and Czerny and all— and over me. What can I do about it? When I was introduced, he asked me to play something. I should have liked to hear him first, but knowing how Herz plays, I pocketed my pride and sat down. I played my E minor [concerto], which the Rhinelanders . . . and all Bavaria have so raved about. I astonished Kalkbrenner, who at once asked me was I not a pupil of Field, because I have Cramer's method and Field's touch—that delighted me. I was still more pleased when Kalkbrenner, sitting down at the piano and wanting to do his best before me, made a mistake and had to break off! But you should have heard it when he started again: I had not dreamed of anything like it. Since then we meet daily; either he comes to me or I to him. On closer acquaintance, he has made me an offer: that I should study with him for three years and he will really make something out of me. I answered that I know how much I lack, but that I cannot exploit him, and three years is too much. But he has convinced me that I can play admirably when I am in the mood and badly when I am not, a thing which never happens to him.

Kalkbrenner's desire to teach Chopin met with strong disapproval from Chopin's family and from Elsner — even if the original purpose of Chopin's travels had been to widen his knowledge and study music further. In Warsaw, everybody, especially Nicholas, felt that although Chopin's only formal piano lessons had been in his early youth under Zywny — he was, in effect, virtually self-taught — he was nevertheless a widely regarded and well thought of pianist who had no need for *three* years extra study.

On Chopin's part, however, there was misunderstanding and indecision: what was his exact destiny to be — a pianist or a composer? He realised only later that his playing and temperament were totally unsuited to the strenuous life of a virtuoso: he could never hope to emulate Liszt, for instance. Elsner, perhaps for different reasons, insisted that Chopin must devote himself to one pursuit — composition — and he argued that Kalkbrenner's offer to teach Chopin would retard his development as a composer, and in any case what worth had a mere 'piano player'? He wanted Chopin to become a great nationalist opera composer, drawing on Poland's past for his inspiration. Yet while Chopin had a deep love for opera, he knew (and Elsner should have) that he was really incapable of developing along such lines, even if the nationalist element was already a distinctive part of his make-up. (Elsner's dream of the nationalist opera composer was never realised in Chopin, and it remained for Moniuszko to later crystallise this vision.)

Chopin expressed his opinions to Elsner in a letter dated 14 December 1831, and tells also of his disillusionment as a composer, his early hopes for success destroyed and his lack of knowledge. At least, he maintained, he still had some small chance and that was as a pianist. If composers like Meyerbeer (a very fashionable musician of the time) had difficulty in finding a platform for their music, what opportunity did he, Chopin, have? He felt that to continue as a pianist was his best decision, although he gave up the idea of studying with Kalkbrenner. 'Three years are a long time, too long; even Kalkbrenner now admits that'. However, this did not disrupt their friendship, and when the E minor Concerto was published in Paris in July 1833, the title page bore a dedication to Kalkbrenner.

Chopin's efforts to become a recognised pianist met with some approval from other young musicians then living in Paris. These included Liszt and August Franchomme, a cellist who became a close friend of Chopin's. Yet in spite of his friendship with these and other ardent romantics, and his contact with the more revolutionary ideals of a progressive artist like Berlioz, Chopin remained aloof and detached in his views. His poetic insight and his sensitive music, often experimental in effect, may have been mistaken superficially for romantic ardour and involvement, but basically he remained indifferent to the ideas, the exuberance and the wholehearted commitment, often political, of his

Louis Philippe
(1773-1850). Lithograph
by François-Séraphin
Delpech

contemporaries. He developed instead along individual lines, independent in concept yet preserving that classical alliegance which was one of the secrets of his art and its survival. He had no sympathy for fashionable trends and with the exception of Liszt's works he never had on his piano any of the exhibitionist trifles composed by the popular pianists of the day.

Paris during these months was still suffering from the effects of the July Revolution, and in a letter to Titus, written on Christmas Day (of 1831), Chopin described his impressions: 'You know there is great distress here; the exchange is bad, and you can often meet ragged folk with important faces, and sometimes you can hear menacing remarks about the stupid Philippe [the king], who just hangs on by means of his ministers. The lower classes are thoroughly exasperated, and would be glad at any moment to change the character of their misery, but unfortunately the government has taken too many precautions in this matter: as soon as smallest street crowds collect, they are dispersed by mounted *gendarmerie'*.

Another of his early experiences in the city was the witnessing of a big public demonstration which lasted from eleven o'clock in the morning to eleven at night.

Many were hurt [he writes in the same letter] '. . . nevertheless a large crowd collected on the boulevards under my windows, joining those who arrived from the other side of the town. The police could do nothing with the surging mass; a detachment of infantry arrived; hussars, mounted *adjutants de place* [military police] on the pavements; the guard, equally zealous, shoving aside the excited and muttering crowd, seizing, arresting free citizens— nervousness, shops closing, groups of people at all the corners of the boulevards; whistles, galloping messengers, windows crammed with spectators (as at home on Easter Day) . . . I began to hope that perhaps something would get done, but it all ended with the singing of *Allons enfants de la patrie* [the Marseillaise] by a huge chorus at eleven at night. You will scarcely realise what an impression these menacing voices of an unsatisfied crowd produced on me.

Chapter 6

Paris II

'His character was not easy to grasp. It was composed of a thousand shades'—Liszt

Chopin's first Paris concert, backed by Kalkbrenner among others, was billed for Christmas Day, 1831, but one of the singers was unable to participate and it was postponed to 15 January. Then Kalkbrenner fell ill and it did not finally take place until 26 February 1832. The setting was the salon of Camille Pleyel, a man 'famous for his pianos and his wife's adventures' (as one contemporary put it). This salon was a large room with a vaulted ceiling, hung with glittering chandeliers, and rich velvet curtains were draped behind the stage. It was without doubt an ideal platform to display Chopin's talents, and the concert launched him into the front rank of pianists in Paris. He offered the F minor Concerto and the *Là ci darem* Variations. No orchestra was available so he played both items as solos, which ideally projected the character of both Chopin and his music. The evening may well have had nostalgic memories for him. He was still homesick, even if not quite to the same extent as before, and the folk rhythms of the concerto's finale, coupled with the painful emotions of the nocturnal slow movement, possibly brought back bitter-sweet memories of his childhood and perhaps Konstancja, too. He may have known of her marriage only a few weeks earlier: she was now lost to him forever.

Chopin also took part in a performance of Kalkbrenner's extraordinary *Grande Polonaise with Introduction and March,* composed for *six* pianos, in which he was joined by, among others, George Onslow, a successful Anglo-French musician, and Ferdinand Hiller. Hiller was a pupil of Hummel and a close friend of Chopin. It was he who had been the first pianist to play Beethoven's Fifth Concerto (the so-called *Emperor*) in Paris.

Chopin's reputation had aroused so much interest in the concert that it was attended by many distinguished musicians and critics. Fétis, the most respected and feared critic of the age, wrote that he found in 'M. Chopin's inspirations the signs of a renewal of forms

The programme
billing of Chopin's first
Paris concert

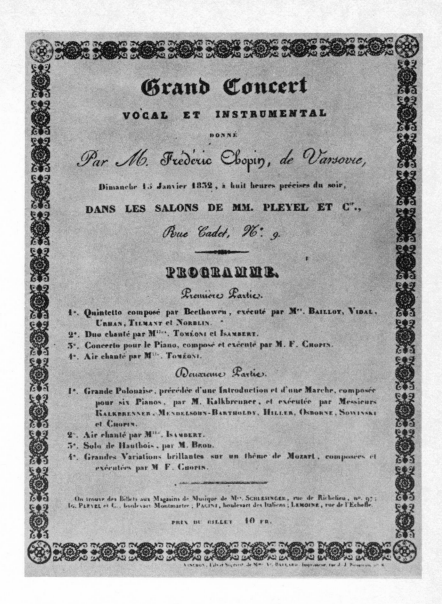

which may henceforth exercise considerable influence upon this
branch of the art' (*La revue musicale,* 3 March). Mendelssohn, on
a visit to the city, was also enthusiastic. One of Chopin's friends,
Anton Orlowski, wrote home to Poland, 'Our dear Fritz has wiped
the floor with all the pianists here: all Paris was stupefied'. Liszt
was transported with admiration. Years later he recalled in his
biography of Chopin: 'We remember his first appearance in the
rooms of Pleyel, where we were so delighted that the most noisy
applause seemed insufficient for the talent that was opening a new
phase of poetic sentiment . . . he was not confused for a moment by
the dazzlement or intoxication of the triumph. He accepted it
without pride and without false modesty'.

Chopin. Portrait by
Teofil Kwiatkowski
formerly attributed to
Rubio (Alfred Cortot
Collection)

This was incidentally one of Liszt's earliest contacts with Chopin and in the event it was to mark the beginning of a friendship between the two men that latter-day disciples were soon to ascribe as legendary. It may be noted, however, that the association (which lasted *less* than ten years) was actually a rather one-sided affair. Liszt, the coarser and less refined of the two, assumed the rôle of the ardent admirer while Chopin was wary of his gestures of all-embracing comradeship. And if Chopin respected Liszt's virtuosity, he thought he wasted too much time on worthless trifles: on one occasion he remarked that Liszt knew 'everything better than anyone... he is an excellent binder who puts other people's works between his own covers... he is a clever craftsman without a vestige of talent'. So far as Chopin's relationships with arch-romantics of Liszt's disposition were concerned, it would probably be truer to say that his attachment with, say, Berlioz (whom he met at the end of 1832 and at whose house at Montmarte he was a frequent guest) was on a sincerer level than anything in his

68

The hall of the Paris Conservatoire. Woodcut, anonymous, *L'Illustration*, 1843

association with Liszt. Legends, however, are hard to break...

The success of this first Paris concert, and the hospitable atmosphere of the city, so unlike Vienna, prompted Chopin to give another, and on 20 May he appeared at a charity concert in the concert hall of the Conservatoire, playing the first movement of the F minor Concerto. The occasion was again important but this time the impression on the public was less favourable. The small tone which Chopin produced from his piano failed to compete with the orchestra, and the actual orchestration of the concerto was criticised. Again, it seemed, Chopin was faced with a setback, and he thought of going to England, or even America, which was then enjoying a period of some stability under their president, Andrew Jackson.

Chopin once again wondered at the possibilities of a concert career. With Paris in the grip of a cholera epidemic, and his funds at rock bottom, it was fortunate for him that Prince Valentin Radziwill took him as a guest to the home of the illustrious and immensely rich Baron Jacob Rothschild, youngest son of the most important banking family in 19th century Europe. At long last Chopin found himself accepted and welcomed by a family whose influence was very wide-reaching. Suddenly he was much in demand among the aristocracy. Ten years later he recalled his gratitude to the Rothschilds by dedicating his Fourth (and last) Ballade to the Baroness Charlotte de Rothschild.

The material gain of this new friendship was that Chopin emerged as a fashionable teacher: his refined background made him more acceptable than the average teacher of his day and he enjoyed the patronage of all the principal families in Paris, whose daughters he was to teach for practically the rest of his life.

Although his own formal training had been slight, Chopin's methods as a teacher were sound and useful. He insisted that all his pupils practise Clementi's set of 100 studies called *Gradus ad Parnassum,* and for gaining independence of fingers he found

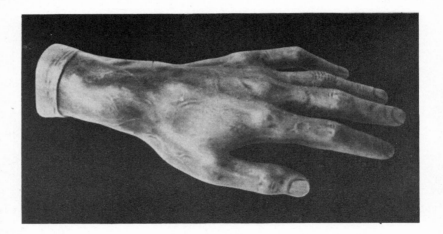

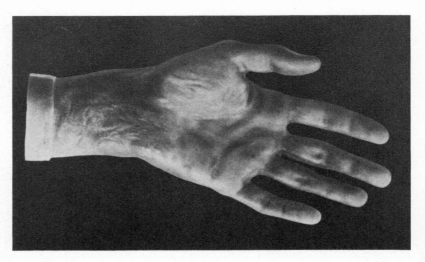

Chopin's left hand. Modelled by Clésinger, 1849

70

Bach's preludes and fugues from the *Forty Eight* 'indispensable'. More advanced pupils also learnt his own works such as the studies. In playing scales he preferred to begin with that of B major as this gave a good hand position; until this was perfected he would not teach other scales, and he regarded the white-key scale of C major as the most difficult to execute properly. He considered three hours' practise sufficient if a student was not to get tired or bored with the music, and he always looked for a pure, unforced tone, and a perfect *legato* touch when required. In interpretation he disliked the unnecessary exaggeration and dramatic effect so admired by his contemporaries. His choice of fingering was often unorthodox if this helped gain greater fluency and *cantabile,* and he was among the earliest teachers to realise the benefit of a psychological approach in teaching his pupils; that is to say, he always considered the individual needs and differences of various students.

For his lessons, he received a fee of 20 francs, about 6 guineas today, left on the mantlepiece, but he charged more when he gave private lessons in the homes of his pupils. He generally gave five lessons a day, yet it is strange to think now that, while his example influenced many, he had practically no pupil who developed professionally as a musician to carry on his tradition (unlike, say, Liszt whose students were famous).

As a teacher he soon became rich and by 1832 had moved into a luxury apartment:

> I am in the highest society: I sit with ambassadors, princes, ministers and even don't know now how it came about, because I did not try for it. . . Though this is my first year among the artists here, I have their friendship and respect. One proof of respect is that even people with huge reputations [for example, Pixis and Kalkbrenner] dedicate their compositions to me before I do so to them . . . finished artists take lessons from me and couple my name with Field's. In short, if I was not stupider than I am, I should think myself at the apex of my career, yet I know how much I still lack to reach perfection.

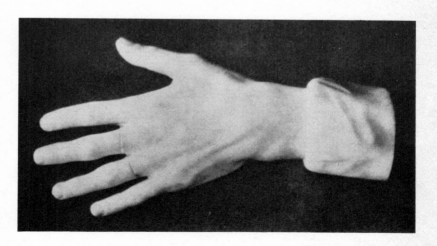

Liszt's left hand.
Plaster cast

He was able to afford his own manservant (unusual for a musician), and a carriage, while his clothes—white gloves and all— came from the best and most fashionable Paris shops: 'without them I should not have *bon ton*'.

The sudden impact which Chopin had made was reflected, too, by publishers anxious to be associated with such a socially popular figure. In December 1832, he had the satisfaction of seeing the publication of the first set of three Nocturnes (Op. 9; the second of these enjoyed a wide success because it was not excessively difficult), two sets of Mazurkas, and the early Piano Trio which he had completed in Warsaw. Compositions in hand included the first six of his second set of piano Studies, Op. 25, which were finally completed in Dresden in 1836, and he began work on the first movement of a new piano concerto. But this never materialised—the music eventually became the rarely heard *Allegro de Concert,* Op. 46, finished in 1841.

During this period John Field visited Paris (having earlier—in February— appeared at a Philharmonic Society concert in London), and Chopin at long last had the opportunity of hearing him play. But unfortunately Field, no longer at his best and in ill

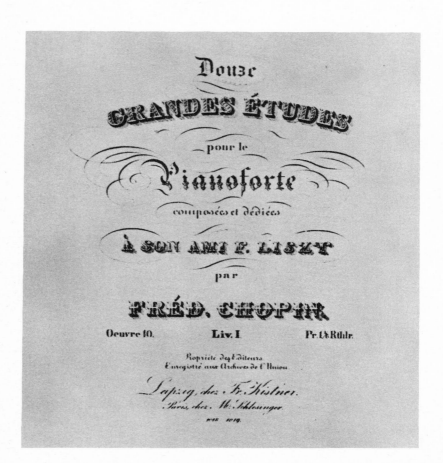

The title page of Chopin's Twelve Studies, Op. 10, from the first German edition, August 1833

health, created a poor impression, and Chopin had little means to judge for himself the touch and technique of a pianist with whom he had been so often and consistently compared.

The flush of success for Chopin continued throughout the following year, 1833. In April he gave a concert with Liszt, and on 20 June he wrote to Hiller 'without knowing what my pen is scribbling because at this moment Liszt is playing my *études* and transporting me outside my respectable thoughts. I should like to steal from him the way to play my own *études*'. The following month this monumental first set of Studies was published by the Paris firm of Schlesinger, with the inscription on the title page, 'Douze Grandes Études pour le pianoforte composées et dédiées à son ami F. Liszt par Fréd. Chopin'. The E minor Concerto was issued at the same time.

In December a second set of Nocturnes (Op. 15) was published, and on the 15th of the month Chopin joined Liszt and Hiller at the Conservatoire in a performance of Bach's Concerto for three pianos. During 1833, too, Chopin became friendly with Bellini, whose Italian operas and melodic style he admired.

1834 was a fairly uneventful year. Chopin gave no important concerts, and his only excursion from Paris was with Hiller to attend the Lower Rhineland Music Festival, held in Aachen in May. Here he renewed his friendship with Mendelssohn, who wrote to his mother (23 May):

> . . . when I was coming up [after a rehearsal of Handel's oratorio, *Deborah*] who should stumble right into my arms but Ferdinand Hiller, who almost hugged me to death with joy. He had come from Paris to hear the oratorio, and Chopin had left his scholars in the lurch, and had come with him, and thus we met again. I had now my full share of delight in the Musical Festival, for we three lived together, and got a private box in the theatre (where the oratorio is performed), and of course next morning we betook ourselves to the piano, where I had the greatest enjoyment. They have both improved much in execution, and, as a pianist, Chopin is now one of the very first of all. He produces new effects [pedalling, for example], like Paganini on his violin, and accomplishes wonderful passages, such as no one could formerly have thought practical. Hiller, too, is an admirable player—vigorous and yet playful. Both, however, rather toil in the Parisian spasmodic and impassioned style, too often losing sight of time and sobriety and of true music; I, again, do so perhaps too little—thus we all three mutually learn something and improve each other, while I feel rather like a schoolmaster, and they a little like *mirliflores* or *incroyables* [French dandies]. After the festival we travelled together to Düsseldorf, and passed a most agreeable day there, playing and discussing music; then I accompanied them yesterday to Cologne. Early this morning they went off to Coblenz *per* steam—I in the other direction—and the pleasant episode was over!

Among Chopin's works published in 1834 were the Fantasia on Polish Airs, the Krakoviak and the fashionable Grande Valse Brillante (Op. 18). He also completed seven of his second set of

Felix Mendelssohn
(1809-47). After the
portrait by C. Jäger

twelve piano Studies. Amongst them were the well known *Butterfly* study and the tremendous Allegro con fuoco *étude* in B minor, a piece notable for its terrifying succession of double-octave passages, which Hans von Bülow (who later became Liszt's son-in-law) once described as an 'Asiatic wilderness'. It was the first time Chopin had penned such an extended display of octaves, and one feels that Liszt might well have been the inspiration behind this torrent of virtuosity.

Contrary to popular belief, Chopin was always interested in the other creative arts. As a member of the Polish Literary Society in Paris, he found time to keep abreast of both artistic and political developments in his homeland, and was a keen student of Polish literature, then unknown in purely French circles. So for Chopin, as for all Polish exiles during these years, 1834 must have been chiefly memorable for the publication of Adam Mickiewicz's national epic, *Pan Tadeusz*. Victor Hugo once wrote that 'to speak of Mickiewicz is to speak of the beautiful, the just, the true; is to speak of the cause whose soldier he was, of the duty whose hero he was, of the liberty whose apostle he was, of the deliverance whose forerunner he was'. In *Pan Tadeusz*, Mickiewicz painted such a powerful picture of Poland, its traditions and spirit, its past and present, that for those Poles under Russian domination it brought back almost tangible memories of the freedom they had once known. For exiles like Chopin it evoked an atmosphere, a beacon of faith, which became embodied in the pulse and soul of his music.

Adam Mickiewicz (1798-1855). Portrait by Henryk Rodakowski (Mickiewicz Museum, Warsaw)

Chapter 7

Interlude

'In vain did I give a ring'—Witwicki

In April 1835 Chopin gave his last two public concerts in Paris. Their failure finally decided him against furthering his career as a concert pianist. His temperament and intimate approach to the piano were at variance with the young *Klaviertiger* of the day, and he found the element of such competition distasteful. In any case his success as a teacher and composer was steadily growing, and at heart this was Chopin's real desire.

At the first of the concerts, on the 4th, he offered the E minor Concerto and played a duet with Liszt. The public response was lukewarm, but a few weeks later, on the 26th, he summoned up enough enthusiasm to give the first performance of his Grande Polonaise for piano and orchestra in the vaulted, box-lined concert hall of the Conservatoire. This had been written several years previously, but Chopin had recently added a quiet, nocturnal *Andante spianato* for solo piano by way of a prelude. The success was only moderate: after this concert he occasionally played to private gatherings but made no attempt to seek engagements as a pianist.

He was now able to devote more time to composition. The well known Fantaisie Impromptu was written (though not published until 1855, several years after his death), together with various *brillante* concert waltzes and some mazurkas. he also finished his first official set of Polonaises (Op. 26), two dramatic pieces in minor keys. During these months the First Scherzo was published by Schlesinger, and in August of 1835 his English publishers, Wessel & Stodart, who had premises at 1 Soho Square, brought out their own edition. The owner of the firm, Christian Rudolph Wessel, came originally from Bremen in Germany, and had started the company in 1825. An astute business man, he saw the potential in Chopin's work at a time when many ignored it, though he is reputed to have paid only about £12 for each new composition, and his provision of fanciful titles of his own invention for each piece enraged Chopin. In several cases,

Above. Maria Wodzińska
(1819-96). Self-portrait,
1835
Below. Clara Schumann,
née Wieck (1819-96).
After the lithograph by
Eduard Fechner, 1832

however, he managed to get out his own editions of the music before the French or Germans, no mean feat.

It was during August that Chopin met his parents for the first time since leaving Poland. They were in Carlsbad for a month's holiday, and Chopin wrote to Louise in Poland: 'I can't collect my thoughts or write anything but our happiness at being together at this moment. To think that what I had so long only dared hope for has today come true, and happiness, happiness, happiness is here!'

Carlsbad was a beautiful health spa (it still is), situated along the banks of the Ohre river: to the north rose the peaks of the Ore Mountains, while some way to the south the great expanse of the Bohemian Forest stretched down to the Danube. For a brief moment in time Chopin forgot all his earlier troubles, the magic of his childhood flooded back, and he found himself in a state of almost unreal bliss. He little knew then that when his parents returned to Warsaw on 14 September, he was never to see them again.

Soon afterwards Chopin renewed his friendship with the Wodziński family. They had left Poland during the 1831 revolt, and in 1835 were visiting Dresden for the summer months, although their home was in Geneva. As a child Chopin had spent many happy hours with the sons of the family who lived in the Chopin household when they were studying at the Lyceum. The Wodzińskis also had a daughter, Maria, and Chopin was astonished to find that she had matured into a young woman of rare beauty and attraction. Since his experiences with Konstancja, Chopin had been cautious in his emotional life but he found a chord of sympathy in Maria and fell for her charms. She was a good pianist — good enough, in fact, to later play one of Chopin's ballades at a public concert in Warsaw — and he wrote for her the A flat waltz (Op. 69, No. 1) which she later called *l'Adieu*. Maria's mother realised Chopin's feeling for her daughter and did not discourage them. Others noticed, too, and one old friend wrote to Louise: 'Oh, we know Maria has won his heart . . .'

On 26 September Chopin left Dresden for Leipzig. At the home of Friedrich Wieck, a renowned pianist and teacher, he met Mendelssohn and, for the first time, Schumann. Wieck's daughter, Clara, later married Schumann. She admired Chopin's music and style of playing and as early as July 1832 (it will be recalled) had performed the *Là ci darem* Variations at an Akademische Musikalen in Leipzig. Chopin once described her as 'the only woman in Germany who can play my music'.

Mendelssohn left a vivid account of the visit in a letter (6 October) to his sister, Fanny:

I cannot deny, dear Fanny, that I have lately found you by no means do him [Chopin] justice in your judgement of his talents; perhaps he was not in a humour for playing when you heard him, which may not infrequently be the case with him. But his playing has enchanted me afresh, and I am persuaded that if you, and my

77

father also, had heard some of his better pieces, as he played them to me, you would say the same. There is something thoroughly original in his pianoforte playing, and at the same time so masterly, that he may be called a most perfect virtuoso; and as in music I like and rejoice in every style of perfection, that day was most agreeable to me. . .

It was so pleasant for me to be once more with a thorough musician, and not with those half virtuosos and half classics, who would gladly combine in music *les honneurs de la vertu et les plaisirs du vice*, but with one who has his perfect and well-defined phrase; and however far asunder we may be in our different spheres, still I can get on famously with such a person, but not with those half-and-half people. Sunday evening was really very remarkable, when Chopin made me play over my oratorio [*St. Paul*] to him, while curious Leipzigers stole into the room to see him, and when between the first and second part he dashed into his new études and a new concerto [possibly the *Allegro de Concert* but more likely the E minor Concerto], to the amazement of the Leipzigers, and then I resumed my *St. Paul*—it was just as if a Cherokee and a Kaffir had met to converse. He has also such a lovely new *notturno* [Op. 27, No. 2 in D flat], a considerable part of which I learnt by ear. . . So we got on most pleasantly together, and he promised faithfully to return in the course of the winter, if I would undertake to compose a new symphony and to perform it in his honour.

Chopin. Watercolour by Maria Wodzińska, *c.* 1836

But for Chopin the winter was to be spent in Paris. Unfortunately, he became seriously ill with influenza. He tried to conceal the fact, but no one heard from him and rumours spread that he was dead. This sort of talk was the last thing Chopin wanted the Wodziński family to hear, for obviously they could hardly let their daughter marry a weakling, apparently on the verge of death. Maria seems to have been unconcerned, but her mother viewed the position anxiously.

Nevertheless in the July of the following year (1836), the Wodzińskis invited Chopin to stay with them at Marienbad, another Bohemian spa near Carlsbad, noted for its precisely laid out grounds and the gently sloping hills which surrounded the town. Chopin accepted the invitation, and August was spent with Maria. They made music and had long country walks: for Chopin it was a time of comparative happiness. When the Wodzińskis left for Dresden in early September, Chopin followed. Here he composed the exquisitely flowing study in A flat which opens the second set of Studies, and also a song called *The Ring*. This was after a poem by Witwicki and its lines—like those of the same poet's *The Sad Stream* which Chopin had set some years earlier—seem to reflect the sum total of Chopin's feelings and thoughts. One senses that he sees in this the fate and inevitability of his future with Maria: perhaps, too, on the threshold of a momentous decision he looks back wistfully to the memory of Konstancja:

. . . and I already loved you,
and for your left little finger
a silver ring I gave you.

Others have married girls
I faithfully loved;
there came a young lad, a stranger,
though I gave a ring.

Musicians were invited
at the wedding I sang!
To another you became a wife,
I still loved.

Today the girls jeered at me,
bitterly I wept:
in vain have I been faithful and constant,
in vain did I give a ring.

This was written on the 8th. The following day at the 'grey hour' (twilight) Chopin proposed to Maria. She accepted, but her family intervened and placed Chopin on probation for a period of good behaviour. In particular he had to avoid late nights in the salons of the Paris nobility: 'keep well, everything depends on that'.

Chopin left on the 11th, and passing through Leipzig he spent the day with Schumann, playing parts of his, as yet, unfinished Second Ballade, which bore a dedication to Schumann. In return

Robert Schumann
(1810-56). Portrait,
anonymous, *c.* 1835

Schumann inscribed his *Kreisleriana,* written two years later, to Chopin. Chopin also played the first two *études* from his second set. Schumann recalled in the *Neue Zeitschrift für Musik:*

> Let one imagine that an Aeolian harp had all the scales and that an artist's hand had mingled them together in all kinds of fantastic decorations, but in such a way that you could always hear a deeper fundamental tone and a softly singing melody—there you have something of a picture of his playing. It is wrong to suppose that he brought out distinctly every one of the little notes: it was rather a billowing of the chord of A flat, swelled here and there by the pedal ... When the study was ended you feel as you do after a blissful vision, seen in a dream, which, already half-awake, you would fain recall ... and then he played the second, in F minor ... so charming, dreamy and soft, just as if a child were singing in its sleep.

Ever since reviewing the *Là ci darem* Variations, Schumann had held Chopin in high regard, and once even began to write a set of variations on one of his nocturnes (the G minor from Op. 15). Only the previous year he had penned a sensitive little musical portrait in the *Carnaval* cycle. Chopin, however, could never quite bring himself to accept, or reciprocate, the gushing friendship which Schumann, like Liszt, showed, nor could he confide in Schumann the secrets, tragedies or joys of his life. He had little enthusiasm for Schumann's fantasies or the schizophrenic nature of his music, and in later years Schumann's relationship with him began to dwindle and finally ceased altogether. The lukewarm nature of Chopin's own feelings for Schumann is well illustrated by the fact that when the Second Ballade was published, the dedication was simply to '*Mr*. Robert Schumann' (*cf.* the Op. 10 Studies). In truth he always remained a lone figure. He shared his confidences with few, and would-be friends found it difficult, if not impossible, to break through his aristocratic reserve.

Back in Paris Chopin soon forgot Madame Wodzińska's advice, and resumed his carefree social life. But as winter gripped Paris, so

Autograph manuscript of the Second Ballade, the ending; the inscription at the conclusion is in another hand (Bibliothèque du Conservatoire de Musique, Paris)

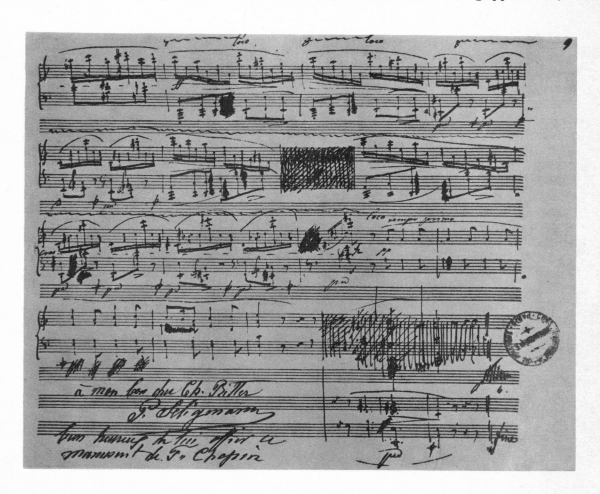

his health deteriorated, and he was forced to take to his bed, again — ostensibly — with influenza. The Wodziński family made up their minds: Maria could not marry Chopin. She had no say in the matter, for her life and affairs were controlled by her parents, as was the custom, and she could not question or protest against their wishes. As Chopin recovered, he wrote letters to them and sent presents but the gestures fell on barren ground for the Wodzińskis did not reply. Finally, when they did, Chopin could not mistake the tone of their letters: as far as they were concerned he had failed his 'probationary' period. He resigned himself to his fate, and bundled together his letters and memories of Maria, simply writing on them (in Polish) 'my miseries'. They remained among his possessions for the rest of his life and although he got over the disappointment, his music for a while reflected something of his depression.

This was particularly so in such works as the impassioned Second Scherzo with its strong contrasts of storm and calm, and the famous Funeral March which was later incorporated into the Second Piano Sonata. Another interesting (if slight) work of the time was Chopin's contribution to an anthology of variations on the March from Bellini's last opera, *I Puritani*. This collection appeared under the title *Hexameron* and was originally commissioned by the Princess Christine de Belgioioso in aid of Italian refugees. Raymond Lewenthal phrased it well when he wrote that the music 'had no pretension or intention of doing anything but entertaining a crowd of rich patricians who were to be relieved of a considerable sum of money for a worthy cause', and he summed it up as 'an omnibus of musical styles, Paris 1837, a microcosm of some aspects of Liszt and one of the most interesting historical documents from the wild and woolly days when pianists were composers and composers were pianists'. Liszt's involvement was extensive but the individual variations were no less full of character and identity: apart from Chopin's quiet whisper

'My miseries'

there were contributions from Czerny and Thalberg as well as Herz and Pixis, two especially popular *salon* composers of the period.

It was during these months that Chopin gained a valuable new friend in Charles Hallé, then aged seventeen. Of German extraction, Hallé, later to become first Principal of the Royal Manchester College of Music, lived in Paris between 1836 and 1848 and his letters home make nostalgic, evocative reading and particularly in their sometimes intimate references to Chopin:

Hexameron, the title page

> The same evening I went to dine with Baron Eichthal, where I was very cordially treated, and where I heard—*Chopin*. That was beyond all words. The few senses I had have quite left me. I could have jumped into the Seine. Everything I hear now seems so insignificant, that I would rather not hear it at all. Chopin! He is no man, he is

HEXAMERON.

MORCEAU DE CONCERT.

Grandes

VARIATIONS DE BRAVOURE

pour Piano

sur la Marche des PURITAINS de Bellini.

Composées

pour le Concert de Mme la Princesse Belgiojoso au Bénéfice des pauvres

par MM.

LISZT, THALBERG,

PIXIS, HENRI HERZ, CZERNY & CHOPIN.

an angel, a god (or what can I say more?). Chopin's compositions played by Chopin! That is a joy never to be surpassed . . . Kalkbrenner compared to Chopin is a child. I say this with the completest conviction. During Chopin's playing I could think of nothing but elves and fairy dances, such a wonderful impression do his compositions make. There is nothing to remind one that it is a human being who produces this music. It seems to descend from heaven—so pure, and clear, and spiritual. I feel a thrill each time I think of it. If Liszt plays *still better*, then the devil take me if I don't shoot myself on the spot (2 December 1836).

Later, in his *Autobiography*, Hallé was to give us a pen-sketch of Chopin the man:

With greater familiarity my admiration increased, for I learned to appreciate what before had principally dazzled me. In personal appearance he was also most striking, his clear-cut features, diaphanous complexion, beautiful brown waving hair, the fragility of his frame, his aristocratic bearing, and his princelike manners,

Charles Hallé (1819-95), aged thirty-one. After the painting by Victor Mottez

singling him out, and making one feel the presence of a superior man. Meeting often, we came into closer contact, and although at that time I never exhibited what small powers I might possess as a pianist, he knew me as an ardent student, and divined that I not merely admired but understood him. With time our acquaintance developed into real friendship, which I am happy to say remained undisturbed until the end of his too short life.

The winter and spring behind, Chopin made a fleeting fortnight's visit across the Channel in the July of 1837, a few weeks after the young Victoria had been crowned Queen. Together with Pleyel he went to Windsor, a fashionable spot on the Thames: punts frequented the river and open carriages were seen in the Great Park. The sights of London were 'done' and both Chopin and Pleyel were depressed yet fascinated by the dankness of the Tower. They also visited Blackwall (famous for its fish dinners) and Richmond. On this occasion Chopin had no wish to make his presence known but he did consent to play once at the London house of the English piano manufacturer, James Broadwood, the

Windsor Castle and the Thames. Steel engraving by Henry Winkle (from *Eighty Picturesque Views on the Thames and Medway*, London, *c.* 1835)

The Tower of
London. Steel engraving
by Henry Winkle (*ibid*)

Liszt. Portrait by
Henri Lehmann
(Carnavalet Museum,
Paris)

son of John Broadwood, one of whose pianos had been sent as a
famous gift to Beethoven in 1817.

Back in Paris in October the second set of Studies, Op. 25, was
published with a dedication to the Countess Marie d'Agoult who
was then living with Liszt. The Liszt-d'Agoult affair had long been
a talking-point of Parisian society, and, though it was becoming
sour and unhappy, it provided as much diversion for a
gossip-orientated public as the exploits of Madame Pleyel or Lola
Montez. Chopin, as yet an innocent, may have disapproved but
himself was soon to fall in to the same situation. One of the
strangest and most colourful personalities of the day, and a woman
whose influence on him was to be cataclysmic, was about to enter
his life. Her name? George Sand.

Chapter 8

George Sand

'. . . sketches, the beginnings of studies . . . ruins, eagle's feathers . . .'
—Schumann on the *Préludes*

George Sand, baptised Aurore Dupin, was born in 1804. Married at eighteen, her husband, Casimir Dudevant, was a dull, unimaginative man who cared little for his young and strong-willed wife. For a time she reconciled herself to this situation and in their spacious country mansion at Nohant (in the Berry region of France, some 180 miles south of Paris, where she had been brought up as a child) she made every effort to please him. She even stopped playing music 'because the sound of the piano drove you away'. Casimir, it appears, remained unmoved and the marriage soon disintegrated into one of convenience. The consequences were predictable if slow to materialise. After nine years Sand revolted and in 1831 came to Paris where she suddenly found that she could mix freely with musicians, writers and painters. Here there were no inhibitions: their enthusiasm for life was hers to share. An independent, forthright streak began to distinguish her character. To her mother she wrote: 'What I want is not society, noise, theatres, clothes . . . it's liberty. Here [in Paris] I can go out when I like, at ten o'clock or midnight, that's my business'. As the years passed so these traits were to become more pronounced.

1831 marked not only Sand's arrival in Paris (as well as, of course, Chopin's) but also the beginning of her career as a novelist and playwright. If her literary talent was overshadowed by the example of such great contemporaries as Hugo, Balzac, Lamartine and Stendahl, her books nevertheless enjoyed a wide popularity, although in England she acquired the reputation of being an evil writer and a disrupter of family unity. Her subjects ranged from the sentimental *Indiana**, through the social observation of *Lélia,* to simple rusticity as in *François le Champi*. All in all she wrote some eighty books, some of an autobiographical

George Sand
(1804-76), at thirty.
Painting by Delacroix,
1834

*This was published in 1831: it was the first of her works to bear the pseudo-nym—George Sand—which was taken from the name of Jules Sandeau, a novelist and one Sand's first lovers.

Victor Hugo
(1802-85). Engraving by
James Hopwood

Baron Casimir
Dudevant. Sketch by
Maurice Dudevant-Sand
1840

nature, and many of which were dramatised with varying degrees of success. Her philosophy reflected to a large extent that spirit of emancipation and revolt against established order which was characteristic of the 1830s and after. It contained, too, an element of independence stemming directly from Sand's reactions as an individual in a materialistic world which in many respects was socially less advanced than the ideals to which she aspired.

Sand was a close friend of Liszt and his mistress, the neurotic, possessive, embittered and vindicative Countess Marie d'Agoult, and one day in the autumn of 1836 she went to one of the Countess's renowned *soirées* at the Hôtel de France where the musical and literary celebrities of the day regularly met. Chopin was apparently invited, too. This was his first meeting with Sand. Six years younger and just engaged to Maria Wodziński, he was seemingly repelled by the image of Sand: yet on 13 December he sent an invitation for her to attend a *soireé* which he was giving. One of the guests, Josef Brzowski, described the occasion:

> Madame G. Sand, dark, dignified and cold. . . Her dress fantastic (obviously proclaiming her desire to be noticed), composed of a white frock with a crimson sash and a kind of white shepherdess's corsage with crimson buttons. Her dark hair parted in the middle, falling in curls on both sides of her face and secured with a ribbon around her brow. Nonchalantly she took her place on the sofa near the fireplace, and, lightly blowing out clouds of smoke from her cigar, answered briefly but seriously the questions of the men sitting beside her. . . After Liszt and he had played a sonata, Chopin offered his guests ices. George Sand, glued to her sofa, never quitted her cigar for a moment.

Even after this occasion, Chopin could not quite bring himself to accept Sand and what she represented, though by now he was increasingly fascinated by her outspoken beliefs and practices. Nevertheless when she invited him to spend the spring of 1837 at her country estate, with Liszt and Marie d'Agoult, he declined. His relations with the Wodziński family were already difficult, and matters could clearly only worsen, or collapse altogether, if they thought he was associating with so notorious a woman as Sand, even though she was by now legally separated from her husband and free to pursue her own goals in life.

If Chopin was becoming more attracted to Sand, the same was true for her. Although she continued to have liaisons with minor artists, and may even have had some success with Liszt, Chopin posed a challenge which she was anxious to conquer. Yet in spite of his appearance as the refined, slightly built dandy — then highly fashionable — Sand did not dominate him. As Mickiewicz once said about the Sand-Chopin *affaire*, 'Chopin is her evil genius, her moral vampire, her cross'. Such a balance was preserved almost throughout their relationship.

During the summer of 1838, following appearances at the French court in February, and in March at Rouen (when he

Marie d'Agoult
(1805-76). Painting by
Lehmann, 1840

offered, once again, the E minor Concerto), Chopin began to see more of Sand. By now his engagement with Maria Wodzińska was broken off, and he found that with Sand he could confide and express those innermost emotions which he had for so long harboured secretly for Maria and once before for Konstancja. Soon, however, social gossip made Paris a less desirable refuge for Chopin and Sand, and they became anxious to be free and together, away from prying eyes and malicious talk. The opportunity presented itself when Félicien Mallefille, one of Sand's ex-lovers (whom she had discarded for Chopin), sent Chopin a eulogy 'as a proof of my affection for you and my sympathy for your heroic country'—little realising that Chopin himself was now Sand's lover. When the truth emerged, a duel became imminent, and one day as Sand was leaving Chopin's apartment, her incensed ex-lover chased her down the street. Chopin found this distasteful. Clearly he and Sand must leave Paris. She was in agreement, and since her fifteen-year-old son, Maurice, was ill with rheumatism, she used this as an excuse to take a holiday in a warmer climate, in Majorca in fact. She left Paris on 18 October accompanied by her eight-year old daughter, Solange. Chopin followed separately,

Chopin. Pencil
drawing by Jakob
Goetzenberger, October
1838

Maurice Dudevant-Sand (1823-89). Portrait by Luidi Calamatta (Carnavalet Museum)

together with his treasured volumes of Bach, plenty of manuscript paper, and several unfinished works, including seventeen of the set of twenty-four *Préludes,* Op. 28, which he had begun in 1836. He had sold them to Pleyel (to whom they were dedicated) for 2,000 francs, some of which was loaned to Chopin to help defray the costs of his departure.

Chopin, looking 'fresh as a rose and rosy as a turnip', joined Sand at the end of October in the old, once Moorish city of Perpignan, in the Pyrénées. Originally the capital city of the Spanish kingdom of Majorca, it was a rather sleepy town, relieved and dominated by the Gothic cathedral of St. Jean, and the medieval castle which had offered in the past a home and a citadel to the kings of Majorca. The atmosphere was quite different from anything which Chopin had ever encountered. He had not sensed such a spirit of adventure and new worlds since his first journeys away from Poland as a child. With Sand, he travelled down the Mediterranean coast to Barcelona, and at five o'clock on the evening of 7 November, they boarded the *El Mallorquin,* an early steamship which also relied on a schooner rig to guide it on its way should the engines ever fail. They were formally registered as 'Mme Dudevant [George Sand], married; M. Maurice, her son, minor; Mlle. Solange, her daughter, minor, and M. Frédéric Chopin, artist'. In her diary Sand left an atmospheric description of the voyage to Palma on the island of Majorca:

> The night was warm and dark, illuminated only by an extraordinary phosphorence in the wake of the ship; everybody was asleep on board, except the steersman, who, in order to keep himself awake, sang all night, but in a voice so soft and subdued that one might have thought that he feared to awake the men of the watch, or that he himself was half asleep. We did not weary of listening to him, for his singing was of the strangest kind. He observed a rhythm and modulation totally different from those we are accustomed to, and seemed to allow his voice to go at random, like the smoke of the vessel carried away and swayed by the breeze. It was a reverie rather than a song, a kind of careless floating of the voice, with which the mind had little to do, but which kept time with the swaying of the ship, the faint sound of the dark water, and resembled a vague improvisation, restrained nevertheless by sweet and monotonous forms.

Palma. Lithograph by Donnadieu (from Laurens' *Souvenirs d'un voyage d'art à l'île de Majorque,* Paris 1840)

Palma was a quiet, romantic spot. In the haze of the late autumn of 1838, the still waters of the Mediterranean met with long stretches of golden sands, and the harbour walls sheltered a bay, dominated by a towering cathedral, set against a backcloth of receding hills. Majorca was the largest of the Balearic Islands in the western Mediterranean, and had long been under Spanish sovereignty. Since pre-historic times the island had offered a home and a refuge to the Phoenicians, the Greeks, the Carthaginians and the Romans, all of whom had left evidence of their occupation. The great Cyclopean remains — vast walls built from boulders — stood magnificent in their solitude and strength: legend has it that they were built by the Cyclopes, the one-eyed giants of Greek mythology, described by Homer in his *Odyssey* as 'a fierce, uncivilised people, who ... have no assemblies for the making of laws, nor any settled customs, but live in hollow caverns in the mountain heights, where each man is lawgiver to his children and his wives, and nobody cares anything for his neighbours'.

During a later age, Majorca was an outpost of the Moorish Empire and became a hideout for the Barbary pirates, Moslem seafarers who preyed on Christian shipping along the Mediterranean trade routes of medieval times. The beauties of the island were already well known in Chopin's day, but had not yet been spoilt or invaded by visitors. The inhabitants were largely poor, and scratched a living from such pastoral occupations as wine-making, the rearing of sheep and pigs which were sent to the Spanish mainland, or by mining such valuable commodities as marble and copper: in fact they continued to lead a life virtually identical to that of their forefathers centuries earlier.

Chopin and Sand were soon made aware that the islanders offered no welcome to strangers, and preferred to live in their own, closed world. Some rooms above a barrel-maker's workshop offered a noisy contrast with the luxuries of Paris, but Chopin's and Sand's sense of freedom, and their emotional involvement,

Solange Dudevant-Sand (1828-99). Portrait by Mercier (Carnavalet Museum)

93

made them oblivious to such living conditions. Sand was in a gay mood, and after a week (on 13 November) she wrote:

> When you arrive here you begin by buying a piece of land, then you build a house and order the furniture. After that you obtain the government's permission to live somewhere and finally at the end of five or six years [!] you begin to open your luggage and change your shirt, while awaiting permission from the customs to import shoes and handkerchiefs.

A few days later, on the 19th, Chopin sent an enthusiastic letter to Fontana, though communications were so slow (they had only a weekly postal service) and uncertain that it was not received in Paris until after the Christmas of that year:

> I am in Palma, among palms, cedars, cacti, olives, pomegranates, etc. Everything the *Jardin des Plantes* has in its greenhouses. A sky like turquoise, a sea like lapis luzuli [a particular shade of blue], mountains like emerald, air like heaven. Sun all day, and hot; everyone in summer clothing; at night guitars and singing for hours. Huge balconies with grape-vines overhead; Moorish walls. Everything looks towards Africa, as the town does. In short, a glorious life! Love me. Go to Pleyel: the piano has not yet come. How was it sent? You will soon receive some Preludes. I shall probably lodge in a wonderful monastery, the most beautiful situation in the world: sea, mountains, palms, a cemetery, a crusader's church, ruined mosques, aged trees, thousand-year old olives. Ah, my dear, I am coming alive a little. I am near to what is most beautiful. I am better.

The couple soon moved to a villa in Establiments, a village near Palma. It was a small, plain white-washed square house with shuttered windows and a flight of crumbling steps leading to the door. It was called 'Villa son Vent' (House of the Wind), and although it was primitively furnished no one seemed to care. In

The Villa son Vent.
Drawing by Maurice
Dudevant-Sand

Valdemosa.
Lithograph by
Donnadieu (*ibid*)

particular the weather, although already November, was as warm
as Paris in summer, and it proved a tonic for Chopin's health. He
went on long country walks with Sand and her children, and one
day they made their way to a lonely spot on the seashore which
could only be reached by a rough goat track leading down the
craggy cliff face. For some years Chopin's health had been suspect.
It finally broke down when, on the way back home from this
excursion, a violent gale blew in from the sea and buffeted Chopin
so much that his lungs were weakened. In one sense it was perhaps
the turning point of his life, for he never recovered completely
from the effects of this damage. His acute bronchitis, and the poor
living conditions in the house, became magnified when the
weather deteriorated and winter set in. Torrential rains nearly
flooded the villa, the bare plaster walls swelled with the rising
damp, and a dank chill settled. A charcoal stove, with
overpowering fumes, was the sole protection against the elements.
Chopin's cough grew steadily worse and in a letter, written to
Fontana from Palma on 3 December, he sketched in something of
his predicament. In the face of such illness his humour was
remarkable:

95

I have been as sick as a dog these last two weeks; I caught cold in spite of 18 degrees of heat, roses, oranges, palms, figs and three most famous doctors of the island. One sniffed at what I spat up, the second tapped where I spat it from, the third poked about and listened to how I spat it. One said I had kicked the bucket, the second that I am dying, the third that I shall die.

It is scarcely surprising that with these symptoms a rumour of consumption (from which, it will be recalled, Chopin's youngest sister, Emilia, had died many years before) spread through the village, with the owner of the villa demanding exorbitant compensation and a costly disinfection for his apparently 'soiled' summer house. Conditions for Chopin and Sand had suddenly become desperate, particularly as their rooms in an old, deserted Carthusian monastery at Valdemosa, were not yet ready to occupy. The monastery was an isolated place, set among forested mountains, and Sand and Chopin had come across it during one of their early trips through the island. Two years previously the last

Valdemosa, the monastery. Lithograph by Donnadieu (*ibid*)

monks had been disbanded by government order, and the monastery left empty and silent. The cells opened out into a small, walled garden, wild and overgrown, below which, stretching down the valley, were terraces of vineyards and orange and almond trees. The surrounding mountains curved together in a protective wall, broken to the south by a gap through which the distant waters of the Mediterranean could be seen on a clear day. Sand was captivated by this desolate haven of natural beauty (15 November):

> I have . . . reserved a cell, i.e. three rooms and a garden, for thirty-five francs a year in the monastery of Valdemosa—a huge and splendid deserted convent in the mountains. Our garden is strewn with oranges and lemons: the trees are cracking beneath their burden. . . Vast cloisters of the most beautiful architecture, a delightful church, a cemetery with a palm tree and a stone cross like the one in the third act of *Robert le Diable* [an opera by Meyerbeer]. The only inhabitants of the place, besides ourselves, are an old serving-woman and the sacristan—our steward, door-keeper and *major-domo* [a Spanish word signifying the master of the house] rolled into one. I hope we shall have some ghosts. My cell door looks on to a huge cloister, and when the wind slams the door, it rumbles like gunfire through the convent. You see that I shall not lack poetry and solitude.

It was arranged that Sand and Chopin would finally take over the cells and furniture (from a Spanish political refugee and his wife) on 15 December. Chopin, of course, was still a very sick man, yet, only the day before, Sand wrote that 'he is recovering, and I hope he will soon be better than before. His goodness and patience are angelic. We are so different from most of the people and things around us . . . our family ties are only more strengthened by it and we cling to each other with more affection and intimate happiness'.

How wise, however, it was to move to Valdemosa was something which neither Sand nor Chopin seem to have thought about. The monastery was exposed to high winds and bad weather. Damp, clinging, rain-laden mists rolled in from the sea, and the sun seldom emerged from behind the winter clouds, save occasionally late in the mornings, appearing momentarily from the shoulder of one mountain to disappear behind the next. But in spite of lack of comforts and food, Chopin seemed heartened with his new surroundings and he made an effort to enjoy himself. A few days after Christmas he wrote to Fontana:

> Palma, 28 Dec[ember] 1838
> . . . or rather Valdemosa, a few miles away. It's a huge Carthusian monastery, between the rocky cliffs and the sea, where you may imagine me without gloves or haircurling, as pale as ever, in a cell with such doors as Paris never had for gates. The cell is the shape of a tall coffin, with an enormous dusty vaulting, a small window; outside the window, orange trees, palms and cypresses; opposite the window, my bed on straps under a Moorish filigree rosette. Beside

the bed is a square and soiled writing desk, which I can scarcely use, and on it (a great luxury here) a leaden candle-stick with a candle. Bach, my scrawls, and another's wastepaper; silence, you could scream, and there would still be silence. Indeed, I write to you from a strange place. . . Nature is benevolent here, but the people are thieves because they never see strangers and so don't know how much to demand. Oranges can be bought for nothing, but a trouser button costs a fabulous sum. But all that is just a grain of sand when one has this sky, this poetry that everything breathes here, this colouring of the most exquisite places, colour not yet faded by men's eyes. No one has yet scared away the eagles that soar every day above our heads!

In the meantime Sand, with whom Chopin was now passionately in love and possessed jealously — although she described her own feelings for him as simply 'maternal' — worked on a new novel, *Spiridion,* and taught the children. They were as wild and free as the birds and revelled in their new surroundings. Maurice was fond of sketching — he later had aspirations to become a painter — and left many drawings of the monastery, its gardens and cemetery, and the surrounding countryside. Sand kept a goat for milk, prepared all the meals and generally tried to create a homely atmosphere. Although she joined the children on their rambles, and was once seen at the theatre in Palma, she was concerned mainly in working on her book, while Chopin composed, secure in the knowledge that she was near to him. His health made it impossible for him to leave the monastery, and he grew increasingly morbid and disturbed when left alone. According to Sand, Valdemosa had become for Chopin a place full of hidden terrors and phantoms.

Ironically, when Sand and Chopin had planned to visit Majorca, one of their main intentions had been to further their artistic experiences. Almost every factor was against them. Chopin's dreams of writing new works was only realised partially. His Pleyel piano was held up in transit and did not arrive until the middle of January (1839), and he was compelled to use a very much inferior local upright. The Op. 28 *Préludes* were finally completed and he sent them to Fontana on 22 January, asking him to give them personally to Pleyel. Although much of the set was already written before the Majorca period, at least four were actually written on the island, one of which (in E minor) at the end of November, at the time when Chopin fell ill. It was later transcribed for the organ, and played at Chopin's funeral service. If there are moments in Chopin's music when one senses that each note is a meaningful reflection of his innermost thoughts and moods, then this prelude is just such an example, one of his saddest utterances, crystallising and holding suspended in time a fragment of his despair. On the same sheet of paper as this prelude, Chopin also sketched the series of mournful and strange progressions which make up the prelude in A minor, as well as the E minor mazurka, published later as part of the Op. 41 set.

Among the many legends, mostly false, which have come down to us, one in particular is associated with the *Préludes*. Sand related in her *Story of My Life* how one day she returned to the monastery after a heavy storm, and heard Chopin playing one of his *Préludes* against the monotonous accompaniment of rain drops falling from the eaves. As we know, Chopin disliked stories being fitted to his music and Sand says that 'when I called his attention to those drops of water which were actually falling upon the roof he denied having heard then. He was even vexed at what I translated by the term, imitative harmony. He protested with all his might — and he was right — against the peurility of these imitations for the ear. His genius was full of mysterious harmonies of nature'. Which prelude Sand heard Chopin playing has never been discovered. Some have suggested the one in B minor with its slow, deliberate pulse and the repetition of one note in the right hand part, but it is usually thought to be the one in D flat major, which is now nicknamed popularly the *Raindrop* Prelude. Here the same persistent note is maintained in regular quavers from beginning to end, passing through an oppressive procession of images: 'the shades of the dead monks seem to rise and pass before the listener in solemn and gloomy funeral pomp' (Sand).

It is significant — if we accept that Chopin's moods were sometimes embodied in the pages of his music — that with the

Valdemosa, the old cemetery. Drawing by George Sand (Aurore Lauth-Sand Collection)

Cimetière de Valdemosa 7bre 1839

exception of the short Prelude in B flat major, a ray of sunlight piercing dark clouds, Chopin's efforts on Majorca were primarily subjective essays, almost entirely melancholic, inward looking and tormented in their colours and emotions. A good example is the tragic cast of the Polonaise in C minor, which the Russian composer Anton Rubinstein (who founded the St. Petersburg Conservatoire) once likened to the downfall of Poland, an analogy which can just as easily be applied to Chopin since for him the essence of life and death was so often inexorably intertwined with the spirit and fortunes of his homeland. It is interesting to observe, too, that Chopin's powerful bass theme in the *minor* key looks back to the optimistic *major* key theme of Kurpiński's *Coronation* Polonaise, written in 1825; it will be recalled that Chopin got to know this composer at the Warsaw Conservatoire, and actually quoted one of Kurpiński's tunes in his own Fantasia on Polish Airs. The image which Rubinstein evokes may assume too great a subtlety of thematic transformation on Chopin's part (though it is not beyond the realms of possibility that in his particular frame of mind Chopin would have resorted to such a sad thematic mutation), but there is no denying that it its gloom and drama the C minor Polonaise offers a striking contrast with its hopeful companion, the A major Polonaise, written in October *before* leaving for Majorca. A harsh reality had replaced the earlier idyll.

More storm clouds loomed over the horizon in the dramatic gestures of the C sharp minor Scherzo (No. 3), which was begun in January 1839, and finished in the summer of that year, with a dedication to Chopin's close friend and pupil, Adolf Gutmann. Gutmann was nine years younger than Chopin, and was reputed to play the first chord of the scherzo so powerfully as to 'knock a hole in the table'. The turbulence of the music seemed to recall stresses

El Mallorquin. Pastel

Genoa. Painting,
anonymous (from
Wiszniewski's *Podróz do
Wloch, Sycylii i Malty*,
Warsaw 1848)

which had long been absent, and these violent episodes are
punctuated by a sonorous, chorale-like melody, subsequently
decorated with cascading showers of notes, almost programmatic
in implication no matter what Chopin's negative views were on
extra-musical imagery. There seems little doubt that in the end,
the environment in which Chopin found himself — the
·inhospitality of the people, the isolation of his existence, the effect
of the poor weather on his health — coloured much of his thought
and influenced his actions, until finally he was almost totally
obsessed by his predicament.

He and Sand decided to end the 'complete fiasco', and as the
winter rains ceased they made plans to leave the island.
Unfortunately the trip to Palma was so rough that Chopin suffered
a lung haemorrhage. By the time they boarded a ship on 13
February — again the *El Mallorquin* — Chopin was decidedly the
worse for wear, and did not take kindly to the heavy seas during the
crossing to Barcelona, or the load of live pigs which the ship
carried as cargo. On arrival in Barcelona they were transferred to a

Chopin in Marseilles,
May 1839. Sketch by
Maurice Dudevant-Sand

French ship where Chopin received proper medical attention; he was by then a pitiful wreck of the happy adventurer who had left this same port for Majorca a few months previously.

After resting for a week, Chopin and Sand made their way to Marseilles. Here Chopin recovered quickly, and his correspondence, especially to Fontana, began to reveal an alert business mind: no longer the young, inexperienced composer anxious to sell his work to the first prospective buyer, he could now afford to be selective and dictate his own terms.

As soon as he was better, Chopin endeavoured to share Sand's life more fully. He encouraged her to take an interest in Polish literature, and translated for her the writings of Mickiewicz. With typical enthusiasm she wrote an essay, 'Goethe, Byron and Mickiewicz', which Chopin declared to be 'magnificent .. one must read it. It gladdens the heart'.

Although Chopin preferred to keep his presence in Marseilles quiet, he did make one public appearance on 24 April, at a memorial service for his friend, the French tenor, Adolphe Nourrit, who in a state of delirium had committed suicide on 8 March.

During May, Chopin and Sand paid a brief visit to Genoa, a city with memories for Sand who had eloped there in 1833 with the poet, Alfred de Musset. From Genoa she and Chopin made a gradual journey back to her country house at Nohant where they arrived in June to be among friends again, and to enjoy the summer warmth and the pastoral life of the Berry countryside.

The years Chopin was to spend at Nohant culminated in his development as a composer: these years were, in the best sense, his swan song.

Nohant, the grounds.
Drawing by Delacroix
(Carnavalet Museum)

Chapter 9

Swan Song

'The wonderful originality of his genius'—Hallé

At first Chopin was enchanted with Sand's Louis XVI-style house and estate. To his childhood friend, Wojciech Grzymala, he wrote, 'the village is beautiful: nightingales and skylarks', and the peace of the surrounding countryside—a locale frequently reflected in Sand's own writings—must have offered a welcome relief to the nightmarish experiences of Majorca. One modern writer, Eleanor Perényi, has left a memorable picture of the place:

> It was a plain, handsome manor house without pretension: the main gates faced the village square and the garden, at that season scented with white lilac, was informal. Imperfectly standardised shrubs stood in tubs on the terrace; shaggy archways of vine bordered the lawn; an old tower housed the flock of noisy doves. A farm belonged also to the property, and woods abounding in wild strawberries; nearby flowed the Indre, one of those ravishing miniature rivers that bind the landscape of central France like so many ribbons.

Chopin's own friends were no less evocative in their recollections. The painter Delacroix wrote (in 1842): 'This is a delightful place... every now and then there blows in through your window—opening on to the garden—a breath of the music of Chopin who is at work in his room, and it mingles with the song of the nightingales, and the scent of roses'. In her *Memoirs* Marie d'Agoult recalled 'a promenade along the Indre, the length of the woody path, across the meadows covered with forget-me-nots, nettles and English daisies, climbing many rustic fences, meeting with families of geese and herds of cattle majestically ruminating...' Sand herself remarked, 'we lead the same monotonous, quiet, gentle life. We dine in the open; friends come to see us, now one, now another; we smoke and chat, and in the evening when they have gone, Chopin plays to me at twilight, after which he goes to bed like a child at the same time as Maurice and Solange'.

With the security and care which Sand provided, Chopin found the urge to devote his summer months to a burst of creative composition. Yet it is perhaps significant, and indicative of his fundamentally melancholy and withdrawn character, that apart from the languid Nocturne in G major (Op. 37, No. 2), written in July just a few weeks after arriving at Nohant, and the sensitively warm F sharp major Impromptu, his main work was the stormy Piano Sonata in B flat minor to which he added the earlier Funeral March he had written in 1837. This work aroused some hostile opinions when it was published in the May of the following year (1840), and Schumann dismissed it unhesitatingly. Yet it can today be seen as one of Chopin's greatest achievements, a grandly handled piece for which no prose can adequately describe its musical essence or the experiences it seems to embody. It was only Chopin's second attempt at writing a piano sonata, and just how far he had come since composing the First Piano Sonata in C minor, while he was still a student at the Warsaw Conservatoire, can be judged by comparing the two. The B flat minor Sonata was among the first indications of Chopin's true stature as a composer, expressed on a hitherto unprecedented scale.

With the passing of summer, Nohant no longer seemed to offer the same attractions. Chopin longed to return to Paris, to his friends and exiled compatriots, to the social and intellectual milieu to which he had become accustomed for nearly ten years. He made plans to return and Julian Fontana was kept busy arranging his business affairs and finding separate apartments for Chopin and Sand both of whom were anxious to maintain the image of artistic colleagues rather than intimate lovers. In this they were to succeed for few strangers penetrated their secret and even Chopin's parents, if curious, did not appear to suspect anything deeper or more emotional than a close friendship.

Chopin was explicit in his instructions regarding furnishing, locale and contemporary fashion. For instance, in a letter posted from Nohant on 4 October:

Julian Fontana (1810-69). Medallion by Wladislaw Oleszczyński

> I forgot to ask you to order a hat for me from Dupont in your street. He has my measurements, and knows how light I need them. Let him give me this year's fashion, not exaggerated; I don't know how you dress now. Also go in, as you pass, to Dautremont, my tailor on the boulevard, and tell him to make me a pair of grey trousers at once. You can choose a shade of dark grey; winter trousers, good quality, without belt, smooth and stretchy. You're an Englishman [actually of course, Fontana to whom this letter was addressed, was Polish, not English], you know what I want. He will be pleased to hear hat I am coming. Also a plain black velvet waistcoat, but with a tiny inconspicuous pattern—something very quiet and elegant.

Chopin and Sand arrived in Paris in October. They had rooms in the most fashionable part of the city, and were soon immersed in the social rounds of the aristocracy. They enjoyed a measure of family life: Solange used to come home at weekends, while Maurice's artistic inclinations were being developed by Delacroix with whom he was taking lessons.

During the winter season Chopin spent his time teaching and entertaining. He did little composition, however, finding that the atmosphere and solitude of Nohant was more conducive to his musical ideas — one reason for the fact that almost all his music for the next few years was composed during the summer months. His output was, therefore, rather limited and there were a further two reasons for this. Firstly, he took fastidious care over his work and spent much time revising it; secondly, Fontana, his faithful friend and copyist, left for a tour of America in 1841. This left Chopin to fend for himself in the arduous and time-consuming task of making accurate copies of his compositions. Like Mozart, he found too little time to physically write all the ideas he wanted to develop.

Towards the end of 1839 Chopin came into contact again with Moscheles, to whom he played the B flat minor Piano Sonata. Moscheles responded warmly to the music, his attitude evidently changed from his criticism of earlier years. A few days later they played together at the French court in the Palace of Saint-Cloud,

The Palace of Saint-Cloud. Painting by Constant Troyon (Carnavalet Museum)

and Chopin received a great welcome. In addition to being a pianist, conductor, composer and writer, Moscheles was also the editor — together with Fétis, one of Chopin's first supporters in Paris — of a *Piano Method,* an elaborate publication in three parts, the last of which was devoted to original studies by different composers. The final part of the *Method* appeared in the late summer of 1840 from the Berlin publishing house of A. M. Schlesinger: it included the *Trois Nouvelles Études* which Moscheles had invited Chopin to write, as well as a *Morceau de salon* by Liszt, and a piece composed by Mendelssohn in 1836 (the Étude in F minor).

The year 1840 was spent in Paris, chiefly because George Sand's play, *Cosima,* produced at the Comédie Française in April, had proved a failure, and she could not afford the cost of living at Nohant and inviting guests for the summer. The stay in Paris did not encourage Chopin to compose anything of significance, and it wasn't until the autumn and winter of 1840-41 that he sketched the brilliantly original and innovatory F sharp minor Polonaise, and the Third Ballade, works which helped consolidate the impression made by the so-called *Funeral March* Sonata. Both were finished at Nohant in the summer of 1841. The more dramatic of the two was the polonaise, which Liszt (in his Chopin biography) was moved to describe in the following terms:

> . . . the central section could be likened to the first glimmer of a winter dawn, dull and grey, the tale of a dream after a sleepless night, a dream-poem where impressions and objects unfold with strange incoherencies and strange transitions . . . The principal motive of the polonaise itself has an ominous air, like the hour before the hurricane; desperate exclamations seem to fall upon the ear, a defiance hurled at all the elements. . .

The Collège de France. Woodcut by Dieudonné-Auguste Lancelot (from Joanne's *Paris illustré,* Paris 1863)

Hector Berlioz
(1803-69). Drawing by
Prinzhofer, Vienna, 1845

Another major work of this period was the Fantasy in F minor, completed in May 1841, an example of Chopin's art and inspiration at its most striking and concentrated.

Socially, 1840 was a comparatively uneventful year, highlighted only once in December when Chopin and Sand attended Mickiewicz's course of lectures on Slavonic literature at the Collège de France, where Mickiewicz was Professor of Literature, a post he held until 1844. Two other important events had little direct effect on Chopin. The tenth anniversary of the July 1830 revolution was marked with a spectacular ceremony in which the remains of those patriots who had lost their lives for the cause of the revolution, were re-interred beneath a memorial column in the Place de la Bastille. In commemoration of the occasion, Chopin's friend, Berlioz, was commissioned to write his *Symphonie Funèbre et triomphale.* It was scored for colossal instrumental forces with choirs, and like the earlier Requiem Mass—a work which finally established Berlioz's fame in Paris—symbolised the spirit of *la gloire* with which the French people had so long identified themselves. It was music of the very greatest splendour and dignity, encompassing a collective worship of the national ideal, a glorification of *La France,* the motherland. The Symphony was conceived for the vast spaces of the open air, and it was so performed with an additional military band of two hundred musicians. In his *Memoirs,* Berlioz said that he wished to 'recall the famous Three Days' conflict amid the mournful accents of a solemn march accompanying the procession; to follow this by a sort of funeral oration, or farewell address to the illustrious dead, while the bodies were being lowered into the tomb; and finally to sing a hymn of praise as an apotheosis when, after the sealing of the tomb, the attention should be concentrated on the column alone, surmounted by the figure of Liberty, with her wings outstretched to heaven, like the souls of those who had died for her'.

Later in the year, on 15 December, the remains of Napoleon (whose nephew, Louis Napoleon Bonaparte—later Napoleon III—had tried earlier that year to seize power, only to be imprisoned for his failure to do so) were brought back to French soil from the British island of St. Helena, where he had died in exile in May 1821. They were re-buried in the monumental surroundings of Les Invalides, and Mozart's *Requiem* was sung, a work heard rarely in the Paris of those days, and not to be played again until Chopin's own funeral.

During 1841 Chopin gave a semi-private concert on 26 April in Pleyel's salon before a selected audience of the aristocracy, friends, and pupils, who paid as much as 20 francs (about 6 guineas) for each ticket. He shared the programme, as was the custom, with the soprano Laure Cinti-Damoreau, one of the stars of the Opéra Comique, and the violinist Heinrich Wilhelm Ernst, who as a young man endeavoured to imitate the peculiarities and technical style of Paganini. Chopin received a brilliant reception. The editor of *La France Musicale* wrote:

Lizst. Daguerrotype
c. 1841

Chopin is a composer from conviction. He composes for himself and performs for himself. . . In truth nothing equals the lightness, the sweetness with which this artist preludes on the piano; moreover nothing can be placed beside his works, full of originality, distinction and grace. Chopin is a pianist apart, who should not be and cannot be compared with anyone.

The most colourful review, however, came from Liszt in *La Gazette Musicale,* a paper founded by Fétis. Liszt chose to concentrate less on Chopin, and more on the glamour, the social success and the atmosphere of the concert. In this sense it can hardly be improved as a reminder of concert life in the 1840s for artists of Chopin's celebrity:

Last Monday evening at eight o'clock the salons of M. Pleyel were brilliantly lighted; a ceaseless stream of carriages deposited at the foot of the steps, carpeted and decked with fragrant flowers, the most elegant ladies, the most fashionable young men, the most famous artists, the richest financiers, the most illustrious lords, the élite of society—a complete aristocracy of birth, wealth, talent and beauty.

An open grand piano was on the platform; crowding around, people vied for the closest seats; composing themselves in anticipation, they would not miss a chord, a note, an intention, a thought of him who was about to sit there. And they were right to be so greedy, attentive, and religiously wrought up, for the one they waited for, the one they wanted to see, hear, admire, and applaud was not only a skilled virtuoso, a pianist expert in the playing of notes—he was not only an artist of great renown—he was all this and much more, he was Chopin.

. . . In Monday's concert Chopin had chosen by preference those of his works farthest removed from the classical forms. He played neither concerto nor sonata, nor fantasy, nor variations, but *préludes, études,* nocturnes and mazurkas. Speaking to a society rather than to a public, he could safely show himself as what he is: a poet, elegiac, profound, chaste and dreaming. He had no need to astonish or to shock; he sought delicate sympathy rather than noisy acclaim. Let us say at once that this sympathy was not lacking. With the very first chords he established an intimate communication between himself and his audience. Two *études* and a ballade had to be repeated, and but for fear of increasing the fatigue already obviously betrayed in his pale countenance, the crowd would have demanded again every piece on the programme. 89A

This represents a fraction of a much longer review; in spite of its praise its tone upset Chopin, and there was a sudden and marked cooling of his already luke-warm friendship with Liszt. During the summer at Nohant he gave several intimations of his growing dislike of Liszt and what he stood for. On 13 September he remarked to Fontana:

Liszt's article on the concert for Cologne Cathedral greatly amused me. And 15,000 persons, counted, *and* the president, *and* the vice-president, *and* the secretary of the Philharmonic Society, *and* that carriage (you know what the cabs there are like), *and* that harbour, *and* that steamboat! He will live to be a deputy or perhaps even a king, in Abyssinia or the Congo; but as for the themes of his compositions they will repose in the newspapers. . .

During that summer of 1841 the 20-year old soprano, Pauline Viardot, who was fast making an impressive reputation, particularly in the works of Rossini following her appearance during May 1839 in his *Otello* at Her Majesty's Theatre in London, spent a fortnight with Chopin and Sand at Nohant. Chopin observed that 'we didn't do much music', and this might be interpreted as just one small pointer to the fact that new tensions were beginning to disturb the apparently idyllic calm of previous summers. One such incident was a petty irritation with Solange's governess and music mistress, and Chopin's reaction showed him to be quite the opposite of the timid, weak-willed person so many people had mistaken him for. At this time Solange, who had been brought up irregularly, was becoming excessively spoilt, selfish and undisciplined. Sand wrote her a cautionary letter before she came to Nohant for the summer holidays: 'your brother and I love you but we have no illusions about certain faults which you must correct and which you will surely try to eradicate: self-love, a craving to dominate others and your mad, stupid jealousy'. Yet in spite of these faults Solange always made a special point of trying to please Chopin, and he in turn would try to keep her amused and give her an occasional lesson. He was so annoyed with the attitude of Solange's governess that Sand, not realising the cause of his irritation, wrote (on 20 June):

> He wanted to leave the house. . . I have never had and shall never have any peace with him. . . The day before yesterday he spent the whole day without speaking a word to a soul. Was he ill? Has somebody annoyed him? Have I said something to upset him? I shall never know. . . I must not let him think he is the master here— he would be all the more touchy in future.

The friction which the episode set up was not, however, serious at this stage, and the relationship between Chopin and Sand was on the old footing again by the autumn, when they finally decided to settle down together in the same house in Paris. In December he was invited to play for King Louis Philippe and his court at the Tuilleries Palace, and was given a valuable set of Sevrès porcelain as a token of the occasion.

The music that Chopin produced during this period was characterised largely by those minorial moods of tragedy reminiscent of his earlier years but now invested with a greater sense of maturity and emotional pulse. Particularly typical was the Prélude in C sharp minor, Op. 45, composed between August and September, a work which had nothing to do with the earlier Op. 28 set of *Préludes*. The C sharp minor Prélude was published in November as part of a 'Beethoven Album', a collection of pieces, including Mendelssohn's *Variations Sérieuses*, issued in aid of a fund to build a monument in Bonn to the memory of Beethoven who had died in Vienna in March 1827.

Of more substance were the two Op. 48 Nocturnes (in C minor and F sharp minor), composed by Chopin in October and published the following January by Breitkopf and Härtel in Leipzig, who, anxious to promote the work of Chopin, advertised them as early as December. Schumann reviewed both works in the *Neue Zeitschrift für Musik*, but his admiration, though still faithful, was tinged with certain reservations. He clearly was no longer the slavish admirer, and had become more critical. That his friendship with Chopin was now no longer what it once was is immediately noticeable:

> Chopin may now publish anything without putting his name to it; his works will always be recognised. This remark includes praise and blame; that for his genius, this for his endeavour. . . But, though ever new and inventive in the outward forms of his compositions, he remains the same within; and we are almost beginning to fear that he will not rise any higher than he has so far risen. And although this is high enough to render his name immortal in the modern history of art, he limits his sphere to the narrow one of pianoforte music, when, with his powers, he might climb to so great an elevation, and from thence exercise an immense influence on the general progress of our art.

In 1842, on 21 February, Chopin made another appearance at Pleyel's salon, this time with Pauline Viardot and his friend, the cellist Franchomme. *La Review Musicale* in its review showed itself almost equal to Liszt in the ability to conjure a social scene and to leave an indelible impression of one moment in time:

> Chopin has given in Pleyel's rooms a charming *soirée*, a fête peopled with adorable smiles, delicate and rosy faces, small, shapely white hands; a splendid fête where simplicity was wedded to grace and elegance, and good taste served as a pedestal to wealth. Gilded ribbons, soft blue gauzes, strings of trembling pearls, the freshest roses and mignonettes, in a word, a thousand of the prettiest and gayest hues, mixed and crossed in endless ways on the perfumed heads and silver-white shoulders of the most charming women for whom the princely *salons* contend.

That summer was spent, as usual, at Nohant, and Delacroix joined Chopin and Sand for a time. Using a converted stable for a studio, he painted a portrait of St. Anne, the patron saint of Nohant, which was hung in the village church. Apart from painting he also wrote down some vivid impressions of life at Nohant, though, curiously, he does not mention the colourful village dances which used to take place before Sand's house until they were stopped in 1844. Here Chopin heard many Berry folk tunes played on bagpipe-like instruments. He notated several of them in Sand's music album, and she used some of them in one of her plays, *François le Champi,* when it was performed at the Odéon in Paris during 1849. The little dances which momentarily

Eugène Delacroix
(1798-1863). Self-
portrait (Louvre)

caught Chopin's fancy remained incomplete, unpublished and unperformed until quite recently.*

The most important works of that year were the Polonaise in A flat major, Op. 53, the Fourth Ballade in F minor, and the Fourth Scherzo in E major. Of these the Polonaise is perhaps the best known and represents, with the later Polonaise-Fantaisie, Chopin's culmination of the polonaise genre. His pupil, Gutmann, remarked that 'Chopin could thunder forth in the way we are accustomed to hear it. As for the famous octave passages which occur in it, he began them *pianissimo* and continued them without much increase in loudness . . . Chopin never thumped'. Sir Charles Hallé supported Gutmann's observations when he wrote in his

*Two Bourrees of the period were included in *Chopin: Three Piano Pieces*, edited by the present author (Schott & Co. Ltd., London 1968; Associated Music Publishers Inc., New York City). Joyce Hatto gave them their first performance at the Queen Elizabeth Hall, London 1973.

111

Autobiography: 'I remember how, on one occasion in his gentle way he laid his hand upon my shouder, saying how unhappy he felt because he had heard his *Grande Polonaise* in A flat, *jouée vite!*—thereby destroying all the grandeur, the majesty of this noble inspiration. Poor Chopin must be rolling round and round in his grave nowadays, for this mis-reading has unfortunately become the **fashion**'.

On returning to Paris in November, Chopin and Sand moved into a spacious new residence in the Cité d'Orleans district, and here he was to spend the rest of his years in Paris up to June 1849.

The next important year for Chopin was 1844, and it proved both the climax and the turning point of his life and art. Artistically, the Third Piano Sonata in B minor, completed in the summer, stands as one of his greatest achievements, more serene and less dramatic and tense than the earlier Sonata in B flat minor. Technically, Chopin surpassed himself, and the sonata's triumphal closing bars seem to proclaim a victory both musical and personal. He never again wrote a work of such stature and importance, and although his friends reported that the death of his father in the May of that year left him very depressed, it is significant that in the B minor Sonata we find little reflection of the mood and misery he must have experienced during those months. He had learnt to control his emotions.

In spite of this musical achievement, however, Chopin as a man left much to be desired, and Sand was so disturbed with his philosophy and moods that she wrote to his sister, Louise, inviting her and her husband (who, a recently discovered letter reveals, was bitterly jealous of Chopin's success and fame) to visit Chopin in Paris and later at Nohant during the summer:

> You are bound to find my dear boy very frail and much altered since you saw him last! But don't be too alarmed about his health. It has continued pretty much the same for the last six years, during which I have seen him every day. I hope that with time his constitution will be strengthened, but at least I am sure that with a regular life and care it will last as well as any one else's.

Chopin was elated to be momentarily reunited with his sister and after she left Nohant he recalled in a letter to her: 'Often, when I come in, I look to see if there is nothing left of you, and I see only the place by the couch, where we drank our chocolate... More of you has remained in my room; on the table lies your embroidery—that slipper—folded inside an English blotter, and on the piano a tiny pencil, which was in your pocketbook, and which I find most useful' (18 September).

Later, on the last day of October, Chopin wrote another letter to Louise, and while giving an idea of his life at Nohant, we see another intimation of his dissatisfaction, this time with Sand's son, Maurice, now grown into a determined individual with a highly critical outlook on life. From now on Chopin's days at Nohant were to be numbered:

Chopin's salon at Place d'Orléans 9. Watercolour, anonymous. Chopin's Pleyel is in the corner. Liszt claimed that 'Chopin was fond of Pleyel pianos because of their silvery and somewhat veiled sonority and their easy truth.' Chopin himself once said that when he was in a bad mood he played Érard instruments because of their 'ready-made sound. But when I am in good spirits and strong enough to find the sounds I want I use Pleyel pianos.'

I expect to stay here two or three more weeks. The leaves have not all fallen, only turned yellow, and the weather has been fine for a week; the Lady of the House [Sand] profits by this for various planting and arranging of that courtyard in which, you remember, they danced. There is to be a big lawn and flowerbeds. The idea is to put, opposite the dining room door, a door leading from the billiard room to the greenhouse (what we call an orangery) . . . Sol[ange] is not very well today; she is sitting in my room and asks me to send you hearty greetings. Her brother (courtesy is not in his nature, so don't be surprised that he has given me no message for your husband about that little machine for cigars) is leaving here next month to go to his father for a few weeks, and will take his uncle with him, so as not to be bored.

On the other hand if relations with Maurice were beginning to

Maurice Dudevant-
Sand. Drawing by
Delacroix

break, Chopin still felt confident enough of Sand's support, and in spite of many who claimed that Sand's *Lucrezia Floriani* — written during this period — was a prophetic portrayal of the break-up of life at Nohant, with Chopin and Sand as the central figures in the drama (many of Sand's themes were based on such intimate fact), there is little suggestion in their letters of a lessening of feelings for one another.

1845 passed in much the same way though Chopin's health was now in continuous decline and there was an ever increasing tension between himself and Maurice, with Sand and Solange taking more active rôles in the growing conflict. The addition of a new member to the family — Augustine Brault, a distant relative whom Sand adopted officially in the spring of the following year — did not ease matters. Maurice found her a useful ally. As he matured he showed even less inclination to accept Chopin's offers of friendship, and resented both Chopin's presence and the apparent control which he exerted over Sand; in later years he went so far as to suppress a number of passages in letters between her and Chopin, in a vain effort to deliberately distort the true facts and nature of their relationship. Solange, now in her sixteenth year, tended to support Chopin and disliked Augustine whose humble origins she would recall frequently. Thus in the ensuing family conflict, Maurice and Augustine were set against Chopin and Solange, with Sand standing uneasily between them, at first neutral but increasingly swayed by Maurice's arguments and his scheming designs.

The first major upheaval came during the summer of 1845 when Maurice and Augustine incited the other servant in the house to rise against Chopin's Polish servant, the only person with whom he could talk in his native tongue. In the uproar that followed, a very bitter Chopin had no option but to dismiss his man. As if this wasn't enough the gulf between Chopin and Sand began to perceptibly widen as the growing opposition of their philosophies became more apparent. Chopin, for instance, believed in the governing right of the aristocracy, together with an unquestioning acceptance of the Roman Catholic church and its doctrine (though it must be argued that by the very nature of his association with Sand, he chose to go against the precepts of the Church: here his belief was as flexible as the circumstances demanded). Sand's views on the other hand were totally different. She was disposed towards the common man and his social problems. She wanted a greater democratic existence in which all men had equal rights. She advocated religious freedom. In all this she was, of course, typical of many reformers of her day, and her beliefs were shared by many, and not least by those leaders of the Industrial Revolution in England during the hundred years between 1760 and 1860, a movement which, by its example, prepared the way for the emergence of trade unions. Such ideals anticipated, too, the teachings of the German socialist, Karl Marx, whose *Das Kapital,* which appeared between 1876 (the year of Sand's death) and 1883, embodied the spirit of this movement. Nearer to Sand's own time was Friedrich Engels who had published a book on the working class in England in 1845, and whose epoch-making *Communist Manifesto* appeared in 1848, a year in which revolt and turmoil throughout Europe was yet another expression of the public's reaction against their tyrannical, self-centred overlords.

Sand's beliefs show her to have been a woman of her age passionately concerned with social issues, while Chopin clung to an imperialistic past in which the social structure was on two immovable levels—the ruling class and the servant. Such divided attitudes helped to sever the original bond between Sand and Chopin, and the atmosphere at Nohant became less and less amenable. So much so, indeed, that during 1845 the entire summer passed with Chopin unable to compose a note of music, and it wasn't until the autumn, with the prospect of returning to Paris, that he started work on three important works—the Barcarolle, the Polonaise-Fantaisie and the Sonata for Cello and Piano, written for Franchomme.

In 1846 George Sand began to publish *Lucrezia Floriani* (in serial form): it soon became clear that earlier rumours had been well founded—this really was no more than a flimsy disguise of the actual relationship between Sand and Chopin, though in later years Sand rigorously denied any such resemblance. The book, however, was completed over a period of two years, and it is possible to see how from an opening idyllic bliss, the growing estrangement between Sand and Chopin during this period became more acutely reflected in the pages of her story. The two main characters were Prince Karol, an artist, delicate and refined, whose growing jealousies and personal philosophies finally cause him to kill his mistress, Lucrezia Floriani, an actress no longer young and beautiful. The similarity between Chopin and Sand might have ended there, but Sand went much further in her portrait. Karol, for instance, is six years younger than Lucrezia the same age difference between Chopin and Sand; he is made to have hallucinations reminiscent of Chopin's on Majorca; Lucrezia is seen as an experienced woman with a string of past lovers; she cares little for Karol's religious scruples and encourages social freedom; Lucrezia's son is a replica of Maurice... The similarities could be extended indefinitely. What is especially interesting, however, is that many passages in *Lucrezia Floriani* were later quoted almost exactly in Sand's *Autobiography*—in particular the sections which described Prince Karol in the novel were used subsequently to depict Chopin. Liszt also quoted passages from the novel in his own biography of Chopin, clearly accepting them as the truth and transcribing them without alteration or clarification. There is little doubt that no matter what Sand's protests, both her friends and Chopin's readily saw the connection between *Lucrezia Floriani* and real life, and were increasingly disturbed as each new instalment of the book was published. Whether Chopin at that time recognised himself in

Chopin
Lithograph by
Hermann Raunheim,
c. 1844

Prince Karol is not known; certainly he gave no outward sign of being offended or worried by the content of the novel. In the course of his letters he merely observed that in Paris it 'has aroused less enthusiasm' than Sand's other efforts, and it was not until several years later that he gave any intimation that he was aware of the significance of the book and that Prince Karol and Lucrezia were merely enacting the passing months of his life and Sand's.

Between March 1846 and the late summer of 1847 some of the most incredible scenes took place in the Sand household, all of which helped sow the seeds from which the break between Chopin and Sand sprang. At the end of June 1846 Chopin and Maurice had an argument, and for the first time Sand took her son's side. This action shocked Chopin into a state of disbelief. By September, Sand misread his mood: 'His nerves have calmed down, he has turned the corner and his character has become calmer and more equable'. But in truth Chopin was far from calm and he was reluctant to bring himself to accept Sand's gesture in supporting Maurice. That dreamlike quality which had marked their early years together was irretrievably lost, and this was, significantly, the last summer that Chopin spent at Nohant.

On 11 October he wrote to his family, beginning 'my dearest ones... [sitting] at the table by the piano'. The letter throughout seems to have been a conscious effort to avoid the bigger issues of the moment. There was much comment on the pastoral niceties of life at Nohant, plenty of trivia in general, and some enthusiastic comments on the recent Berlin discovery of the planet Neptune. But in spite of such effort there were still one or two paragraphs which were disturbing in tone. It is these that today give us the nearest clue to Chopin's real frame of mind:

> The whole summer has been spent here on various drives and excursions in the unknown district of the Vallée Noire. I was not *de la partie*, for these things tire me more than they are worth. I am so weary, so depressed, that it reacts on the mood of the others, and the young folk enjoy things better without me... I should like to fill my letter with good news, but I know none, except that I love you and love you. I play a little, I write a little [the summer mainly saw the completion of the Barcarolle, the Polonaise-Fantaisie and the Cello Sonata.] Sometimes I am satisfied with my violoncello Sonata, sometimes not. I throw it into the corner, then take it up again... When one does a thing, it appears good, otherwise one would not write it. Only later comes reflection, and one discards or accepts the thing. Time is the best censor and patience a most excellent teacher.

At the end of that long summer the 18-year old Solange became engaged to Fernand de Préaulx, a young man of breeding and character. By the following February, however, a new suitor had appeared on the horizon: Auguste Jean Baptiste Clésinger, a one-time soldier and now a hard-up sculptor who had first come into contact with George Sand the previous March. Clésinger soon had designs on the strikingly beautiful Solange, and at the last moment she refused to marry Préaulx. A scandal blew up and the family retreated to Nohant with Clésinger in hot pursuit. He seduced

Solange Dudevant-Sand. Bust by Clésinger

Chopin. Pencil
drawing by George
Sand, 1847

Solange and attempted to elope with her. By May the pair were hurriedly married. Chopin was informed at only the last minute, but most of his Parisian associates already knew the nature of the circumstances which had been kept secret from Chopin: 'it does not concern him, and when once the Rubicon has been crossed the "ifs" and "buts" only do harm', Sand wrote to Maurice. If Chopin was upset with Solange — always his favourite — marrying such a vagabond as Clésinger (although Sand made every effort to praise his character), he showed no such signs, and in any case was too ill to involve himself.

Solange had always shown a selfish trait, and this now blossomed to a remarkable degree. In June, Augustine (her distant cousin) became engaged to a friend of Maurice's, Theodore Rousseau. Solange, who had by now discovered that Clésinger was not the ideal husband she had expected (in all fairness she was probably as much a trial for him with her temperament), could not bear to think of Augustine enjoying a happiness denied to her. She let loose a whirlwind of calamity, and it was as well that Chopin was spared the embarrassment of this family feud. Solange fabricated a whole string of lies, first telling Theodore that Augustine had been Maurice's mistress. Sand admonished her, but Solange, torn between hatred and vindictiveness, promptly accused her mother of having an affair herself with another of Maurice's friends. Maurice, back from Holland, could take no more. He attempted to shoot Clésinger but Sand intervened — she did not want a murder on her hands — and punched Clésinger who returned the blow. After such behaviour he and Solange were flung out of the house at Nohant. Clearly things would never be the same again. Solange immediately wrote a false account of the events to Chopin in Paris and asked for the loan of his carriage. Chopin, innocent and little suspecting the truth, replied: 'I am much grieved to know that you are ill. I hasten to place my carriage at your service. I have written to this effect to your Mother'. One can imagine Sand's reaction and fury at the thought that Chopin, very much a helpless victim of circumstance, now appeared to side with Solange against her. Unfortunately, like Chopin, she, too, had little means of knowing either the true position or Solange's treachery. She wrote a violent letter to Chopin which is lost, or else Chopin destroyed it, perhaps in an effort to erase its contents from his mind. Delacroix, who saw it, called it 'cruel' (in his *Journal,* 20 July) and for both Chopin and Sand the damage and insult was irreparable. In spite of Sand's subsequent concern and pleas, Chopin preferred to take Solange's word on the matter and ignored Sand.

Chopin's last encounter with her was in March 1848, but the meeting was little more than an exchange of pleasantries, with no attempt to forget or heal the wound both had suffered. Yet in spite of all this he never forgot her and kept a lock of her hair at the back of his diary to his dying day. In time Sand learned what had really happened, but by then it was too late and although she became reconciled with Solange she neither forgot nor forgave.

Chapter 10

England

'He belonged to those whose charm unfolds especially when they avoid the beaten path'—Liszt

The cataclysmic experiences of the last years at Nohant left Chopin a mentally and physically exhausted man. After finishing the innovatory Polonaise-Fantaisie and the Barcarolle in the summer of 1846, he could only produce a handful of mostly insignificant works, and during 1847 a solitary last song. This had a text by Count Zygmunt Krasiński, a friend of the poet Mickiewicz and himself a poet whose mystical beliefs, allied with a mood of fatalistic resignation and doom, seemed to identify with the gloomy half-world into which Chopin had sunk. Yet in spite of his depression the song remains one of his most inspired and artistically perfect settings of Polish lyrics, with no signs of a falling off of creative powers. Like the B minor Piano Sonata, written against a similar emotional background, it merely consolidates the impression that Chopin in his maturity had learnt to control his emotions: his musical outpourings were now a subtle reflection and no longer an obvious statement of his immediate environment. In the song, Chopin's musical imagery has the subtlety of genius: the warmth and comfort of the opening in the *major* key, gives way to a melancholic outcry in the *minor*. The poet says:

Chopin. Pencil drawing by Franz Winterhalter, 1847

From the hills, where they carried the load of nightmarish crosses,
they saw from a distance the promised land.
They saw light's heavenly rays,
towards which in the valley their tribe was dragging its load,
though some of them will not enter those infinite spaces!
To the comforts of life they will never sit down,
and even, perhaps, they will be forgotten.

The whereabouts of the original manuscript is unknown today, but Chopin is said to have added after the music the 'Nella miseria' from the *Inferno* of Dante Alighieri, lines which perhaps give the best clue to Chopin's emotional trauma: 'There is no greater sorrow than to recall a time of happiness in misery': his spirit was broken, and this song was a last testament.

August
Franchomme (1808-84).
Portrait by
Jean-Auguste-Alfred
Masson

Jane Wilhelmina
Stirling (1804-59).
Lithograph by
Jean-Jacques-Marie-
Achille Devéria

The summer of 1846 had been the last one spent at Nohant, and the following year Chopin was too ill to leave Paris during the summer months which eventually aggravated rather than cured his encroaching illness.

1848 was a year chiefly notable for Chopin's prolonged visit to England, but he began the year with a recital on Wednesday, 16 February, once again in Pleyel's salon on the same stage which had seemed to offer so much promise nearly twenty years earlier. This was to be his last Paris appearance as a pianist. With Franchomme and the violinist Delphin Alard (a professor at the Paris Conservatoire), he played a Mozart piano trio (the one in E major) and the last three movements of his new Cello Sonata. Among his own solo offerings, played in a gentle, restrained fashion, were the Berceuse, the Barcarolle, a nocturne and some waltzes, mazurkas, preludes and studies. He was now so frail that Hallé, one of the privileged few to attend this last recital, tells in his *Autobiography* how Chopin played the Barcarolle 'from the point when it demands the utmost energy, in the opposite style *pianissimo,* but with such wonderful nuances that one remained in doubt if this new rendering were not preferable to the accustomed one'.

Chopin was not deceived by the public's enthusiastic reception. In a letter written to his family a few days before the concert, he shows his feelings:

> . . . my thoughts are occupied with my concert, which is to be on the 16th of this month. My friends came one morning and told me that I must give a concert, that I need not worry about anything, simply sit down and play. All tickets have been sold out for a week, and all are at 20 fr. The public is putting down names for a second concert (of which I am not thinking). The court has ordered 40 tickets, and though the newspapers have merely said that perhaps I will give a concert people have written to my publisher from Brest and from Nantes to reserve places. I am astonished at such *empressement* [eagerness], and today I must play, if only for conscience sake, for I believe I am playing worse now than ever before (11 February).

At this time the political situation in Europe was tense, and Chopin was tempted to accept an invitation from one of his Scottish pupils, Jane Wilhelmina Stirling (to whom he had dedicated his Op. 55 Nocturnes some years before), to visit her and her sister, Mrs. Katherine Erskine, in Scotland. He had serious doubts about the advisability of such a difficult trip in his poor health, but his mind was made up for him when yet another revolution broke out in Paris a few days after his concert.

This was the so-called February Revolution, which was largely the result of public dissatisfaction under the farcical rule of Louis Philippe and the July Monarchy. This government had become increasingly corrupt and autocratic, while those in positions of authority reaped untold benefits at the expense of those who were less fortunate. The anger of the proletariat reached breaking point in the economic crisis and depression of 1846-47 when, ironically through no fault of Louis Philippe's administration, the harvest failed. The February Revolution set the example for a number of similar subsequent uprisings throughout Europe, though ultimately the revolutionaries failed to gain their ideals. In France the direct outcome was the establishment in December 1848 of the Second Republic, with the formerly imprisoned Louis Napoleon Bonaparte as President. This democracy lasted less than four years, and in November 1852 he became known as the Emperor Napoleon III, ruler of the Second Empire, a gesture which reverted to the dictatorial rule of his more illustrious uncle as well as to the autocratic government of Louis Philippe which he himself had ousted.

The outcome of the February Revolution was dramatic. In his *Memoirs* Berlioz left a graphic account of the state that the city had reached by the summer:

Paris, the Revolution 24 February 1848. Oil painting, anonymous (Carnavalet Museum)

Paris is burying her dead. The pavements used for the barricades have been replaced—to be torn up again, perhaps, tomorrow. The moment I arrive I go straight to the Faubourg Saint-Antoine. A hateful scene of destruction; even the Spirit of Liberty on top of the Bastille column has a bullet through her body. Trees mutilated or overthrown, houses crumbling, squares, streets, quays—everything still seems to vibrate under the shock of bloody disorder. Who thinks of art at such a time of frenzy and carnage? Theatres shut, artists ruined, teachers unemployed, pupils fled; pianists performing sonatas at street corners, historical painters sweeping gutters, architects mixing mortar on public building sites. The Assembly has just voted a sum large enough to enable the theatres to reopen and to afford a little relief to the most hard-hit artists. Inadequate relief, above all to the musicians! A first violin at the Opéra was lucky if he earned nine hundred francs a year; he lived by giving lessons. It is hardly to be supposed that he could have saved on a very brilliant scale. Now their pupils have gone, what is going to happen to such people? They won't be deported, though for many of them their only chance of making a living would be in America, India or Sydney. Deportation costs the Government too much. To qualify, one must have deserved it, and our artists all made the mistake of attacking the barricades and fighting against the insurgents.

Chopin's society was no more. His pupils, like everyone else's, had gone. There was a new order of social values. The ideals that George Sand had so passionately championed were beginning to achieve concrete reality. The security of an old order had gone. He was left with few options. He chose, as it were, to escape, if only temporarily. He packed his bags and after a fairly rough sea crossing arrived in Folkestone on the evening of 20 April at six o'clock. After a short rest he reached London the next day, Good Friday, and was met by Jane Stirling and her sister. Within a few days he was settled in a lavishly furnished suite of rooms at 48 Dover Street, just off Piccadilly. His drawing room was large enough to comfortably accommodate three grand pianos placed at

Chopin's Broadwood piano, 1848. In England and Scotland Chopin customarily used a Broadwood at his concerts.

Above. Folkestone. Etching
by S. Widdiman and
William Ellis
Top Right. Jenny Lind
(1820-87). Steel
engraving by
Jacques-Marcel-Auguste
Hüssener
Bottom right. The Hanover
Square Rooms, venue of
the Philharmonic
Society's concerts during
the 1840s. Drawing by
T. H. Shepherd, 1831
(British Museum, Grace
Collection)

his disposal by Pleyel, Broadwood and Érard. He soon found
himself a selection of pupils, amateurs more anxious to call
themselves a pupil of Chopin rather than further any genuine
artistic gifts of their own. His fee was a guinea a lesson, and he
needed it, for his rooms cost him 40 guineas a month, a figure
probably nearer 400 by today's standards. Yet if the cost of living
worried him, he nevertheless had a faithful, if over eager, admirer
in Jane Stirling, who saw to his every need but whose stifling
generosity in the end deprived him of the relaxed atmosphere
which he needed so badly.

Although in poor health, Chopin summoned up enough energy,
to go to the opera, and for the princely sum of two-and-a-half
guineas heard Jenny Lind in Bellini's *La Sonnambula* (at the Hay-
market Theatre). He later met her and observed in a letter (11
May) that she was 'a typical Swede, not in an ordinary light but in
some Polar dawn'. Apart from the opera he also endeavoured to do
the social round of the London aristocracy ('every evening I am
out'), something he was not really fit enough to undertake.

Chopin's letters of these weeks reveal in particularly vivid
terms the atmosphere of the city, and there is again a sense of
that same youthful excitement with his new surroundings which

had characterised his first years of discovery in Paris. To his pupil, Adolf Gutmann, he wrote (on 6 May) that 'all the Parisian pianists come here: Prudent's concert with the Philharmonic [Society] was not very successful; they want classical things here. Thalberg has been engaged for twelve concerts in the same theatre where Lind appears. Hallé is going to play Mendelssohn...' Mendelssohn had died only the previous November, and was all the rage in London: he was then virtually the only foreign composer to command such popularity and respect, a state of affairs helped to no small extent by his standing with Queen Victoria. His music figured prominently not only in the Promenade Concerts of Jullien but also in the programmes of the influential and prestigious Philharmonic Society. Founded in 1813 (they received their Royal charter in 1913) they were then the most important society in the land and their invitation to Chopin to appear at one of their concerts was a singular honour. Chopin, however, declined and many critics, including J. W. Davison of *The Times,* a fanatic supporter of the

Queen Victoria
(1819-1901). Steel
engraving by Mayer
after the portrait by
E. Vaughan

Mendelssohn cult and a much feared writer, were heard to express displeasure at this 'insult'. In a letter to Grzymala (Saturday 13 May) Chopin, however, did not seem especially concerned:

> The day after tomorrow the Duchess of Sutherland is to present me to the Queen, who will visit her *in gratiam* for a christening. If the Queen and Prince Albert, who know about me, should be pleased it will be good, for I shall begin from the top. I have been offered the Philharmonic, but don't want to play there because it would be with the orchestra. I have been there to observe. Prudent played his concerto [on 1 May], and it was a fiasco. There one must play Beethoven, Mozart or Mendelsohn [*sic*], and although the directors and others tell me that my concertos have already been played there [in fact, the F minor had only been played once in 1843, and just two movements of the E minor had been offered the following year], and with success, I prefer not to try, for it may come to nothing. The orchestra is like their roast beef or their turtle soup; excellent, strong, but nothing more. All that I have written is needless an excuse; there is one impossible thing: they never rehearse, for everyone's time is costly nowadays. There is only one rehearsal, and that is in public.

Chopin was presented to Queen Victoria and the Prince Consort at Stafford House (now the London Museum), the home of the Duchess of Sutherland whose daughter took lessons from Chopin. In spite of his success, however, he never actually played for Victoria at the palace, though false rumours (which spread as far afield as Paris) had it that she actually became a pupil of his! In a letter of 19 August to his family (written on three sheets of paper decorated with views of Edinburgh) Chopin left an account of the occasion:

> The Duchess of Sutherland had the Queen to dinner one day, and in the evening there were only eighty persons belonging to the most exclusive London society. Besides the Prince of Prussia (who was to leave London shortly) and the royal family, there were simply such people as old Wellington and so on (though it is hard to find a parallel). The Duchess presented me to the Queen, who was amiable and talked with me twice. Prince Albert an enthusiastic amateur musician and composer came up to the pianoforte. Everyone told me that both these things are rare . . . I should like to describe to you the Duchess of Sutherland's palace but I can't. All the royal palaces and castles are old: splendid, but neither so tasteful nor so elegant as Stafford House (as the Duke of Sutherland's palace is called) . . . for instance, the staircases are famous for their magnificence. They are neither in the entrance nor in the vestibule, but in the middle of the rooms, as if in some huge hall with the most magnificent paintings, statues, galleries, hangings and carpets: of the loveliest design, with the loveliest perspective. On these stairs one could see the Queen, under a brilliant light, surrounded by all sorts of bediamonded and beribboned people with the garter, and all descending with the utmost elegance, carrying on conversations, lingering on various levels, where at every point there is some fresh thing to admire. It is true one regrets that some Paul Veronese could not see such a spectacle, so that he could have painted one more masterpiece.

In the meantime Chopin's sole income was coming from his pupils and from his appearances at the homes of the aristocracy for whom he would play for a fee of 20 guineas, and where he could meet not only the nobility but also men like Dickens, Carlyle and others. With the high cost of living he soon felt obliged to accept almost any engagement. Two private concerts were arranged for 23 June and 7 July, and with seats at a guinea each, he earned about three hundred much needed pounds. The first of the concerts was given at the home of Mrs. Adelaide Sartoris, the daughter of the famous actor, Charles Kemble, but it was less successful than the second one, which took place at the London mansion of Lord Falmouth, at 2 St. James's Square, a house destroyed during the Second World War. Chopin offered a similar programme on both occasions, including the Second Scherzo, the Berceuse, and various other pieces. Pauline Viardot also sang some vocal arrangements of Chopin's mazurkas at the second concert. The London *Daily News* for 10 July commented:

> He [Chopin] accomplishes enormous difficulties, but so quietly, so smoothly and with such constant delicacy and refinement that the listener is not sensible of their real magnitude. It is the exquisite delicacy, with the liquid mellowness of his tone, and the pearly roundness of his passages of rapid articulation, which are the peculiar features of his execution, while his music is characterised by freedom of thought, varied expression and a kind of romantic melancholy which seems the natural mood of the artist's mind.

At the end of July the London season was over. Revolution in Europe made it impossible to travel abroad for the annual summer holidays, and the aristocracy followed the example of the royal family and went to Scotland, at a time of the year which also coincided with the start of the shooting season and so made the prospect of holidays in Scotland that much more attractive. Chopin decided to follow suit, and he had a particularly good guide in Jane Stirling, though he once wrote (to Wojciech Grzymala, 17 July) that 'my Scottish ladies are kind, but they bore me so that I don't know what to do. They want to insist that I shall go to their homes in Scotland. That's all right, but nowadays I have no heart for anything. Here, whatever is not boring is not English'.

An invitation from Lord Torphichen, the brother-in-law of Jane Stirling, provided the necessary excuse to leave London at the beginning of August, taking the train to Edinburgh, via Birmingham and Carlisle. The 407 mile journey took twelve hours in all. After a short rest in Edinburgh ('the exquisite city'), he went to Calder House, the home of Torphichen, in a carriage which had been specially provided. In the letter to his family of 19 August Chopin left a description of Calder House as he first saw it:

> It is an old manor surrounded by an enormous park with ancient trees; you can see only lawns, trees, mountains and sky. The walls are eight feet thick; there are galleries on all sides, dark corridors

Calder House.
An old photograph

with endless numbers of ancestral portraits, of various colours, in various costumes, some Scots, some in armour, some in robes; nothing lacking for the imagination. There is even some kind of red cap [ghost], which appears, but which I have not seen. Yesterday I looked at all the portraits, but I have not seen which one it is that wanders about the castle. The room which I inhabit has the most beautiful view imaginable—towards Stirling, beyond Glasgow, and to the north fine scenery . . . there is nothing I can think of that does not at once appear: even the Parisian newspapers are brought to me every day. It is quiet, peaceful and comfortable. . .

Although Chopin was allegedly on holiday, he still found it necessary to continue giving recitals. Later in the same letter he wrote:

. . . they want me to play in Edinburgh. If it will bring in something, and I am strong enough, I shall gladly do it, for I don't know how to turn round this winter. I have my lodging in Paris as usual, but don't know how to make ends meet. Many persons want me to stay in London for the winter, in spite of the climate. I want something else, but don't myself know what. I will see in October, according to my health and my purse, for an extra one hundred guineas in my pocket would do no harm. If only London were not so dark, and the people so heavy, and if there were no fogs or smells of soot, I would have learned English by now. But these English are so different from

126

the French, to whom I have grown attached as to my own; they think only in terms of pounds; they like art because it is a luxury; kind-hearted, but so eccentric that I understand how one can himself grow stiff here, or turn into a machine. If I were younger, perhaps I would go in for a mechanical life, give concerts all over the place and succeed in a not unpleasant career (anything for money!); but now it is hard to start turning oneself into a machine. It is fine weather here today, so nothing dry can enter my head. The park has a wonderful light on it—it is morning—and I forget everything; I am with you, I am happy, and I shan't think about the winter till it is imperative to do so.

On 26 August he arrived in Manchester to give a 'Gentleman's Concert', billed for the 28th of that month. In 1848 Manchester was a thriving city, one of the original spearheads of the industrial revolution. Built on the ruins of a Roman centre (Mancunium), Manchester was a centre of political reform, particularly in the rise of the Liberal movement in England, but it lacked the cultural atmosphere of Edinburgh, and Chopin found it even sootier, darker and smellier than London. He was fortunate, however, to spend his stay outside the city, at Crumpsall House, the home of one Salis Schwabe, a patron of the arts and a wealthy manufacturer: 'he owns the biggest chimney in Manchester, which cost £5,000'. Crumpsall House no longer exists, and the site is now occupied by a housing estate built during the mid 1930s.

Chopin's contribution of piano solos at this concert was interspersed between popular and mainly orchestral works by Rossini, Verdi and Bellini. The *Musical World* for 9 September had little to say:

> You must pardon me if I venture to say very little of Mons. Chopin's pianoforte playing. He neither surprised me, nor pleased me entirely. He certainly played with great finish—too much so, perhaps, and might have deserved the name of *finesse* rather—and his delicacy and expression are unmistakable; but I missed the astonishing power of Leopold de Meyer, the vigour of Thalberg, the dash of Herz, or the grace of Sterndale Bennett.

Although it was the height of summer, Chopin found little to really enjoy in his life, and he leaves a sad picture of his predicament in a letter of 18 August to Fontana, who was then in London:

> We are two old cembalos on which time and circumstances have played out their wretched trills. Yes, *two old cembali*, even if you protest at being included in such company—that means no disparagement to beauty or respectability. The *table d'harmonie* is perfect, only the strings have snapped and some of the pegs are missing. The sole trouble is this: we are the creation of a celebrated maker, a Stradivarius of his kind, who is no longer there to mend us. In clumsy hands we cannot give forth new sounds and we stifle within ourselves all those things which no one will ever draw from us, all for lack of a repairer. I can hardly get my breath: I am just about ready to give up the ghost . . . I am vegetating, patiently waiting for the winter, dreaming now of home, now of Rome; now of joy, now of grief.

From Manchester he returned to Edinburgh and spent a short time with a Polish doctor 'who has married well, lives in tranquillity and has become quite **English**'. From here he went to **Johnston Castle, eleven miles from Glasgow, and the home of yet** another of Jane Stirling's family. By now the strain of so much travel began to tell, and while Jane Stirling made every effort to see that Chopin was provided with every comfort, and while she vainly tried to re-create the atmosphere that had once existed at Nohant, Chopin was beginning to find her and the company she kept oppressive:

I am cross and depressed, and people bore me with their excessive attentions. I can't breathe; I can't work; I feel alone, alone, alone, although I am surrounded. . . They are dear people, kind and very considerate to me. There are a whole lot of ladies, 70-80 year old lords, but no young folk: they are all out shooting. One can't get out of doors because it has been raining and blowing for several days (letter to Grzymala, 4 September).

Glasgow. Steel engraving by Joseph Swan (from *Picturesque Views on the River Clyde*, Glasgow 1830)

A welcome relief was provided by the visit of Princess Marcelina Czartoryska, one of the Radziwill family and a pupil of Chopin, accompanied by her husband. Chopin remarked, 'I came to life a little under their Polish spirit: it gave me strength to play in Glasgow where some dozens of the nobility assembled to hear me. The weather was fine, and the Prince and Princess also came by train from Edinburgh'.

The Glasgow concert took place on 27 September at the Merchants Hall; Chopin offered his usual programme of shorter, less taxing pieces, and although he included the Second Ballade he no doubt omitted its more difficult sections (a manner of performance that Schumann had already noted over a decade before).

Chopin next went to Keir House, near Stirling. In a letter to Grzymala, dated 1 October, he wrote: 'Perthshire. Sunday. No post, no railway, no carriage (even for a drive); not a boat, not even a dog to whistle to'. The letter continued in a vein now humorous, now despairing:

> . . . the future grows always worse. I am weaker, I can't compose anything, less from lack of desire than from physical hindrances . . . the whole morning, till 2 o'clock, I am fit for nothing now; and then when I dress, everything strains me, and I gasp that way till dinner time. Afterwards one has to sit two hours at table with the men, *look* at them talking and *listen* to them drinking. I am bored to death (I am thinking of one thing and they of another, in spite of all their courtesy and French remarks at table). Then I go to the drawing room, where it takes all my efforts to be a little animated—because then they usually want to hear me . . . then my good Daniel carries me up to my bedroom (as you know that is usually upstairs here) undresses me, gets me to bed, leaves the light; and I am free to breathe and dream till it is time to begin all over again. And when I get a little bit used to it, then it is time to go somewhere else for my Scottish ladies give me no peace; either they come to fetch me, or take me the round of their families (*nota bene*, they make their folk invite them constantly). They are stifling me out of *courtesy*, and out of the same *courtesy* I don't refuse them.

On 4 October he gave an evening recital at the Hopetoun Rooms in Edinburgh and, *à la* Liszt but unusually for the period, bore the main responsibility of the programme himself without the aid of a singer as was the custom of the day. By now winter was fast approaching. Chopin spent a few days at the resplendent Hamilton Palace as the guest of the Duke and Duchess of Hamilton. On the way back to Edinburgh he caught a chill which weakened him even further. He found life too hectic and too attentive: it was rapidly smothering him, both physically and emotionally, and it only encouraged him to make for London at the earliest opportunity. Yet however ill he was, he mustered enough energy to write a letter on the 21st to Grzymala, that is full of devastating sarcasm in the picture he drew of the social life of the English aristocracy as he saw it:

Hamilton Palace.
Steel engraving by
Joseph Swan (*ibid*)

Art, here, means painting, sculpture, and architecture. Music is not art and is not called art; and if you say an artist, an Englishman understands that as meaning a painter, architect or sculptor. Music is a profession, not an art, and no one speaks or writes of any musician as an artist, for in their language and customs it is something else than art: it is a *profession*. Ask any Englishman and he will tell you so. . . No doubt it is the fault of the musicians, but try to correct such things! These queer folk play for the sake of beauty, but to teach them decent things is a joke. Lady —, one of the first great ladies here in whose castle I spent a few days, is regarded here as a great musician. One day, after my piano, and after various songs by other Scottish ladies, they brought a kind of accordion, and she began with the utmost gravity to play on it the most atrocious tunes. What would you have? Every creature here seems to me to have a screw loose. Another lady, showing me her album, said to me, 'La reine a regardé dedans et j'ai été a côte d'elle' [the queen looked in it, and I was beside her]. A third that she is 'la 13me cousine de Marie Stuart' [13th cousin of Mary Stuart]. Another sang, standing up for the sake of originality, and accompanying herself on the piano, a French-English romance. The Princess of Parma told me that one lady whistled for her with a guitar accompaniment. Those who know my compositions ask me, 'Jouez-moi votre *second* Soupir— j'aime beaucoup vos cloches'. [play me your second Sigh—I love your bells]. And every observation ends with 'leik water', meaning

Edinburgh. Steel
engraving, anonymous,
c. 1834

that it flows like water. I have not yet played to any English woman
without her saying to me 'Leik water'!!! They all look at their
hands, and play the wrong notes with much feeling. Eccentric
folk, God help them.

The letter ended with some caricatures, which Chopin was always
so good at drawing, accompanied by such remarks as 'this is a
certain lord in a *collar* and gaiters, stuttering!'
 Chopin returned finally to London on 31 October, and took up
residence for a short while at 4 St. James's Place. Two letters to
Grzymala, dating from November, paint the most dismal picture
of Chopin's situation:

I have been ill the last eighteen days, ever since I reached London.
I have not left the house at all, I have had such a cold and such head-
aches, short breath, and all my bad symptoms . . . I don't care
about anything . . . I have never cursed anyone, but now my life is
so unbearable that it seems to me it would give me relief if I could
curse Lucrezia [George Sand]—but no doubt she also suffers,
suffers all the more because she will doubtless grow old in anger.
I am endlessly sorry for Sol[ange] . . . My kind Scottish ladies are
boring me again. Mrs. Erskine, who is a very religious Protestant,

131

good soul, would perhaps like to make a Protestant of me: she brings me the Bible, talks about the soul, quotes the psalms to me; she is religious, poor thing, but she is greatly concerned about my soul. She is always telling me that the other world is better than this one; and I know all by heart, and answer with quotations from Scripture and explain that I understand and know about it. . . If I were well, with two lessons a day, I should have enough to live comfortably here; but I'm weak: in three months, or four at the outside, I shall eat up what I have (17-18 November).

. . . the London *fogs* are driving me out, so I am returning to Paris, if it is not too late for the journey. My Scotswomen are kind: I have not seen them for two or three weeks, but they are coming today. They want me to stay, and go on dragging round the Scottish palaces . . . wherever I go, they come after me if they can. Perhaps that has given someone the notion that I am getting married; but there really has to be some kind of physical attraction, and the unmarried one Jane Stirling is too much like me. How could you kiss yourself—Friendship is all very well, but gives no rights to anything further. I have made that clear—Even if I could fall in love with someone, as I should be glad to do, still I would not marry, for we should have nothing to eat and nowhere to live. And a rich woman expects a rich man, or if a poor man, at least not a sickly one. . . It's bad enough to go to pieces alone, but two together, that is the greatest misfortune . . . I don't think at all of a wife, but of home, of my mother, my sisters. May God keep them in His good thoughts. Meanwhile, what has become of my art? And my heart, where have I wasted it? I scarcely remember any more, how they sing at home. That world slips away from me somehow; I forget, I have no more strength; if I rise a little, I fall again, lower than ever (undated).

On 16 November Chopin gave what was to be positively his last concert, at a Grand Ball given in the Guildhall, London, in aid of Polish refugees. In no fit state, he played for just an hour and it was appropriate that this final appearance should have linked him again with his exiled compatriots, and with the spirit of the Poland he had known as a child. But this patriotic gesture of Chopin's went unnoticed by all, and he bade farewell to the concert platform without ceremony or acclaim. To those who reported the evening, he was nothing, not even the 'Herr Chopin (piano player)' who had so valiantly tried for his fortune in Vienna all those years before.

Chapter 11

Marche Funèbre

'The whole of this life simply amounts to one enormous discord'—
Delphine Potocka

On 23 November 1848 Chopin left 'this hellish London' for Paris.
By now consumption had claimed him as it had done once before
with his youngest sister, Emilia. No cure was possible and while at
times Chopin's strength appeared to rally, such moments became
increasingly rare. His efforts at composition were feeble. 1848
simply saw copies of an earlier piano arrangement of his Polish
song, *Wiosna* ('Spring'), made first for Sophie Horsley, a
one time friend of Mendelssohn's, and then for Fanny Erskine, a
young girl of about seventeen who seems to have been related to the
Earls of Mar and whom Chopin met at Crumpsall House. In
October he managed to compose a short and still unpublished
waltz for Jane Stirling's sister. He also made efforts during
these last years to write a *Piano Method,* but he made little
progress and the secrets of his art and technique were lost with his
death.

By the spring of 1849 Chopin had moved to Chaillot, a quiet
suburb of Paris, in the hope that the air might do him good ('the
spring sunshine will be my best doctor'), but he soon had to admit
that no matter where he went, in his state of health, Paris was
frightful: 'Thirty-six kinds of weather, plenty of mud, draughts in
the room. Nothing goes: for the moment, everything is disgusting'.
Money was once again becoming an acute problem. He had
seldom had need to save in the past, but now he had few pupils for
he had found it impossible to teach them (realising this, they had
left him for another great pianist-composer who lived nearby,
Alkan). No music had been published since the Cello Sonata in
October 1847, and doctors' fees drained him of his last resources.
In the May he underwent a crisis and burnt some of his
manuscripts. However, the Rothschilds — his first Parisian
benefactors — once again came to the rescue, and in March Jane
Stirling sent an anonymous gift of 25,000 francs (over £5,000 in
those days). Unfortunately this was delivered to Chopin's *concierge*
who hid it in a room, for some extraordinary reason unopened; it

Chopin.
Photograph by L. A.
Bisson, *c.* 1849. This has
often been erroneously
described as a
daguerrotype.

was not until the end of July that it was discovered that Chopin had never received any money. With the aid of a clairvoyant it was found, and while Chopin at first refused to accept it, Jane Stirling's sister, Mrs. Erskine, managed to persuade him to accept 15,000 francs, still a very handsome sum.

In the meantime, Chopin had made a desperate plea to his sister, Louise, to come and visit him: she did, finally reaching Paris on 8 August, accompanied by her husband and daughter. Her husband, Kalasanty Jedrzejewicz, returned to Warsaw soon afterwards, however, and, in view of his bitter hatred of Chopin and his fame and achievement, this was only to be expected. Just how bitter he really was might be realised when it is remembered that Chopin's request to Louise, though written in June, did not reach her until after Jedrzejewicz had it in his possession for *several weeks* and this in spite of its obviously urgent nature. He went so far as to actually refuse to pay the expenses of travelling to Paris, and only agreed to let Louise go if Chopin's mother paid the bill. Eventually Louise, with Isabella and her husband, managed to raise sufficient money but in so doing Isabella and her husband, as well as Chopin's mother, deprived themselves of going to Paris to be near Chopin.

After Chopin's death, Louise, some time in 1853, wrote a 32-page letter to Jedrzejewicz. She never finished it and it remained virtually unknown until it was first published in Warsaw in 1968. A soliloquy, it stands today as a remarkable document and the light it throws on Louise's position and the attitude of Jedrzejewicz, and also of course on Chopin's last months, remains unique. As an intimate statement it can have few parallels:

> You have lost faith in me, yet I never lied to you and you still say you are my best friend. Permit me, my dear, to make a most conscientious confession to you of all my actions, but do believe me, as you once used to, and then you may judge me with your heart and your mind. At the same time I am asking you, if you have still a true friendship and attachment towards me, may this confession remain between us two. . .
>
> When we arrived in Paris Frédéric seemed to have gained a new lease of life, but all the time I saw how many things there used to annoy you, things which it was impossible to change—and I saw how often you were unforbearing to his [Chopin's] little fancies and habits. Granted that it was out of your concern for me, but do admit how many times you were angry with me for sitting by his bed late at night, but many times you reproached him for preventing me from having enough sleep. I know it was dictated by your concern for me, but it was very painful to him, and a great tribulation for me, for I went there to look after him, to nurse him, to console him, to endure any hardship as long as it would bring him even the smallest relief in his sufferings—and he, poor thing, liked to talk late at night, to tell me all his troubles, and to pour into my loving and understanding heart anything that concerned him most. . .
>
> If only you did not become so offended, if only would put yourself in my position—if only you would consider yourself a member of our family and be in harmony with us—if only you had thought of Frédéric as a brother and mourned him together with us . . . you could have come here [for the funeral], helped me and acted to the advantage of us all; but you took offence, no longer remembered who it was who offended you and only thought how to take revenge on me. Judge for yourself if your action was just and noble. . .
>
> . . . on many occasions when I talked to Frédéric and he worried [about money], I asked him to put his mind at ease. . . I told him what my heart was dictating to me but with the knowledge that I would do everything in my power to help him . . .
>
> . . . everybody [in Paris] knew that he [Chopin] had no debts. Since all people adored him and knew about his affection for us and ours for him, they thought it would be best for us to keep all the objects of which the transport would not cost too much, as souvenirs, and to dispose of the rest by selling them to Frédéric's friends. Then I wrote to you and suggested that we keep the piano in the family and in that way have priority over others. To this you replied with one of the most hurtful letters which I ever had in my life: you ordered me to sell absolutely everything (for which you had to send me later a paper giving me authority to sell) and you added: 'sell everything, do not keep anything, anything at all', and 'not one rag [of Chopin's] will I let into my house'. Oh, I wept tears of blood

Louise Chopin.
Daguerrotype

135

over this letter! Can you imagine the pain I felt in my heart, a pain which I had to hide before strangers, because they were glad that I had a letter from you, being sure that your letter must have brought some comfort and relief to my heart. But all I could expect from all your subsequent letters was rubbing salt into my wounds, in spite of that affection which once existed between us. I could not understand you, indeed could you yourself understand your own motives for such tyrannical conduct?

You forbade me to take Chopin's nurse as a travelling companion and told me that you will not accept her into our house. It did not occur to you how difficult it was for me to travel alone with my child, in January, postrate with grief and hardly alive. . .

. . . you became more and more petty. Because [unkind] people told you that I can do with you what I want, you thought that these people had opened your eyes, so you decided to change it. While previously you were the undisputed master of the house now you became an absolute despot. You told our household that nobody else but you had the right to give orders here, that only your will was sacred. It was sufficient for me to be fond of any of the [female] servants to make you dislike her. You told me yourself on many occasions: 'It is enough that you are praising her, she is sure to be useless', and 'As she is your favourite, I must be hard on her'. How did you expect that my orders would be obeyed at home, if after I issued an order the servants would ask me: 'Did the Master order it?' I felt that all these things, painful although they were, did not have their origin in you, but in your offended *amour propre*, and in jealousy fanned by wicked people. Out of a friend you became a tyrant, and I out of a friend became a slave who had no right to ask any questions or to have any say in domestic matters. I could not even talk to you about the children in a manner which becomes parents having confidence towards each other. . .

. . . to all my sufferings one more was added: I ceased to believe in the existence of friendship, and came to the conclusion that God wanted to punish me with this disenchantment. . .

In September, by way of preparing for the winter, a new residence was found for Chopin at Place Vendôme 12, in a roomy, sunny apartment. Chopin's friends visited him: Jenny Lind sang, Delphine Potocka came from Nice, Delacroix stayed, and Solange, whatever her past, seemed to offer a source of hope. From Nohant, Sand made an attempt, in a letter of 1 September to Louise, to learn about Chopin: 'Some people write that he [Chopin] is much worse than usual, others that he is only weak and fretful as I have always known him. I venture to ask you to send me word, for one can be misunderstood and abandoned by one's children without ceasing to love them. . . Your memories of me must have been spoilt in your heart, but I do not think I have deserved all that I have suffered'. Louise never replied.

The year had passed: by October Chopin's health was in such serious decline that the end was imminent. On the 12th he received the Last Sacraments. Five days later at about 2 a.m. in the morning of 17 October 1849, in his 39th year, he died; with **Louise, Solange, Gutmann, and Marcelina Czartoryska at his bedside.**

The funeral service took place on 30 October at the great

Chopin's last
apartment at Place
Vendôme 12.
Watercolour by
Kwiatkowski

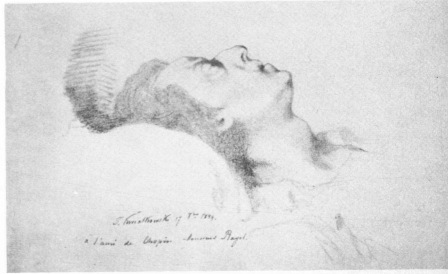

Chopin on his
death-bed. Drawing by
Kwiatkowski

The cemetery of
Père-Lachaise. Steel
engraving, anonymous,
1843

church of the Madeleine. It was an illustrious tribute. In accordance with Chopin's request, Mozart's *Requiem* Mass was sung with Dupont, Pauline Viardot and Castellan, while Lablache (who had sung the *tuba mirum* from the same work at Beethoven's funeral in 1827) also took part. It was an occasion that by all

accounts was spectacular and moving. The artists and nobility of the day were anxious to remember their dead friend in a fashion worthy of his image in life. At the Introit, Chopin's Funeral March from the B flat minor Sonata was heard in an orchestrated version, and his Preludes in E minor and B minor were played on the organ during the Offertory. Meyerbeer (the *première* of whose opera, *Le Prophet,* Chopin had attended in only April) and Prince Adam Czartoryski led the long funeral procession, while the four pall bearers were Prince Alexandre Czartoryski, Delacroix, Franchomme and Gutmann. The procession made its way down the Grands Boulevards to the cemetery of Père-Lachaise. No speech was made at the graveside and Chopin was laid to rest between Bellini and Cherubini. On her return to Warsaw, Louise took an urn containing her brother's heart to be placed in the Church of the Holy Cross—a supremely symbolic and fitting gesture. A year later a monument, designed by Solange's husband, Clésinger, and made possible through a fund set up by Pleyel, was unveiled. It represented a weeping Muse and a broken lyre. A box of Polish earth was sprinkled over the grave.

Chopin's death did not go unrecorded. The *Illustrated London News* for 27 October summed it up well when they began simply, 'One of the greatest celebrities of this musical epoch has just expired in Paris: Chopin is no more'. And they ended: 'He has been styled the *Ariel* of the piano; but he was also its *Prospero*—a mighty magician, inventing imagery, flowing like an impetuous torrent, whilst his hands were a tornado aggregating the subjects and investing them with piquant and picturesque colouring, alternately pathetic and gay, as his fancy dictated'.

Chopin had many imitators but no successor. More than any other composer of his generation he understood and voiced the spirit and ethos of his age, its dreaming, its emotions, its patriotism, its turbulence. His art acknowledged the greatness of his heritage, of Bach and Mozart, and like them he was endowed with a genius that unfolded in strokes of the most direct simplicity and purity. He had no time for conceit or artifice. His music has remained to this day a pageant of experiences and statements as relevant to our understanding of him as a musician as to our awareness of the Romantic era in which he lived.

Chopin was not merely a composer or a pianist: he was also a great visionary artist and lyric poet in whose music the soul of Poland no less than the soul of Europe was transmuted into a unique expression that equally acknowledged both the boundaries of national frontier and the boundlessness of mankind as a universal brotherhood. The fact that his works have stood the test of history so well is perhaps a measure of his immense achievement.

Legends are made, heroes are born. . .

'A man of exquisite heart and . . . mind'—Delacroix

Chopin's death-
mask. By Clésinger.

Index

Illustration pages are indicated by **bold** *figures*